BREAKING THE CYCLE

DAVID M. JOYCE

To Shelly,

DRL
press

David M. Joyce

CONTENTS

TO THE READER

My name is David Joyce, and I am writing this book in the hope that someone will identify with the trauma I have put myself through for most of my adult life, and avoid the psychological, emotional, sociological, and physical damage I have incurred.

I am sixty-two years old and have spent over thirty years of my life incarcerated. I have been to state prisons ten times, in eight different states, and federal prison once. I have been convicted of over forty felonies. I was the definition of a "career criminal." I was a meth addict, who used intravenously, for decades, and I stole to support my drug habit. I was a terrible thief and got caught a lot. At age twenty-three, while incarcerated in the California Department of Corrections, I became a white supremacist, and tattooed WHITE PRIDE on my triceps.

I used to steal wallets from health club lockers, then used the credit cards to purchase items to trade for drugs. Since my crimes were all non-violent property offenses, my sentences were relatively short (2 years, 3 years, 4 years, 5 years). Then, in 1997, I was sentenced to twenty-five years in the Oklahoma Department of Corrections for unauthorized use of a credit card (three strikes). Had I done all the things I was supposed to do, and stayed out of trouble in prison, I could have been out in about nine years. Instead, I decided to escape from prison…twice. After I was arrested for the second escape, in November 2000, I attempted suicide by slicing my throat and wrists with a razor blade.

Fast forward to March 20, 2015, when I was released from the Oklahoma Department of Corrections: I was released with $200 and a bus ticket to California. I was homeless, jobless, and had no transportation. I had no friends, and my family had disowned me years before. I had nothing to put on a job resume, nor could I pass a background check. I had never used the internet, never sent an email or text message. I didn't even have a change of clothes.

Fast forward to today: I have been gainfully employed since five days after my release. I have remained drug free and crime free the entire time. I have been married since April 2017, and have been a faithful and loving husband. I became a homeowner in 2019. I voted for the first time in my life in 2020. I have denounced white supremacy and have permanently covered up the WHITE PRIDE tattoos with black redaction bars.

The past eight plus years have been full of roadblocks and challenges. I was not prepared for life in the real world. I had no marketable job skills and had no recent work history. I didn't know anything about current events and could not participate in most conversations. I didn't know how to be kind and courteous. I felt out of place, like I didn't belong.

Even after eight years, I am still very socially awkward and mainly keep to myself. I live with my wife, Jeri, and three dogs (Little Guy – Yorkie, Buddy – Bassett Hound, and Molly – Yorkie-poo). I have been delivering newspapers for a living for most of the past eight years. I have been mentally ill for a long time, but I have made tremendous progress over the past eight years.

Here is my story…

CHAPTER 1

March 20, 2015 – 8:15 a.m.

"DAVID JOYCE! 2-5-9-7-4-8! REPORT TO CENTRAL CONTROL WITH ALL OF YOUR PROPERTY FOR RELEASE!", blared the PA system at the Oklahoma City Community Corrections Center. When I began this twenty-five year sentence (for unauthorized use of a credit card – 3 strikes) back in 1997, I was housed in maximum security. Seventeen years and eight months later, I had worked my way down security levels, all the way to work release. The problem was that it took me so long to get to work release (because I escaped twice while serving this sentence), I did not have enough time remaining on my sentence, according to my case manager, to go out and look for a real job. My last two months were spent washing dishes at the Oklahoma Highway Patrol Headquarters.

The lieutenant processing me out asked for my forwarding address, and I simply said, "Return to sender." After years of experience, the lieutenant knew I was saying that I was going to be homeless. He was one of the few empathetic correctional officers I had encountered, and asked, "No friends or family?" I told him that all my previous "friends" were drug addicts, and that my family had disowned me years before. In fact, I was able to contact my sister, who was living with our disabled father in Southern California, a couple of months prior to my release, and asked her to ask our father if I could crash on his couch until I found a job. His exact words were: "Don't bring that motherfucker here."

The lieutenant then asked me if I needed a bus ticket. Since I was not required to reside in the state of Oklahoma, I asked for a bus ticket to San Bernardino, California. If I was going to be homeless, I might as well go somewhere warm. I was being released without parole or probation because I had been denied parole each of the three years I went before the parole board prior to my discharge date. He then handed me a debit card with $200 preloaded on it, which was all the money I had in the world.

I was then handed a bill for over $5,000 from the Washington County, Oklahoma, Clerk for court costs, fines, and attorney fees from 1997 when this all began. I had seventy-two hours to set up a payment plan with them, which I did not do, but intended to do if I ever found a job.

Finding employment would be challenging, to say the least. This was not my first felony conviction, nor my first trip to prison. In the thirty-four years between 1981 and 2015, I had racked up over forty felony convictions, and I had been incarcerated for over thirty of those years. The three and a half years I was not incarcerated, I spent shooting meth or cocaine into my veins, and stealing to support my drug habit. I had nothing to put on a job resume, nor could I pass a background check. I had also never been on the internet, and never sent an email or text message. I did not have a copy of my birth certificate or social security card. All I had for identification was my prison ID card. I didn't even have a change of clothes. My chances at success were somewhere between slim and none.

The Transport Officer arrived, and I was driven to the Greyhound station in Oklahoma City, where the officer bought me my bus ticket to California. The officer thanked me for being a long-time customer, got back into his van, and left. For the first time since 1997, I was a free man. No incarceration, no probation, no parole, and no warrants. You'd think I would be happy, but I was more afraid at that moment than I was the day I started this sentence.

Approximately three months prior to my release, I began experiencing extreme anxiety. I'd had this feeling before, but not nearly as intense. All the other times I passed it off as anticipation, or butterflies in my belly, but this time was different. I felt dread. I had trouble eating and sleeping.

When I did sleep, my old nightmares came back. Several times, I woke up screaming, sweating, crying, and trembling. I realized that I was afraid of getting out of prison and told myself I must be mentally ill. Turns out, I was right.

What most people don't realize is that prison does not rehabilitate anyone. There are usually classes and programs available to inmates, such as drug treatment, cognitive/rational behavior classes, anger management, GED programs, etc. These programs do help, but it's the environment itself that is toxic to anyone trying to rehabilitate themselves. For example, prison officials do not like to give inmates responsibility. For security purposes, everything is controlled by staff. They tell you when, where, how, and why (if you're lucky). Inmates get used to being told what to do every step of the way during their incarceration, and when they are released, making their own decisions is not easy.

Another example of prison being a toxic environment is the atmosphere of hate. Every prison in which I have been incarcerated had normalized racism. Though some states are taking steps to reduce racism, virtually every prison I have been to will not house inmates of different races in the same cell. (In county jails, however, inmates of different races are routinely housed together.) This is to prevent a racist attack on someone who is sleeping and cannot flee. When first timers come in, someone from their own race will talk to them about the rules that were not in the rule book they were given by staff. Everyone, from every race, is told the same thing: stick with your own race. There are very few gray areas in prison. Prison staff are usually okay with this, as there are fewer racial incidents.

When a person does anything for a long enough period of time, whether good or bad, what they are doing becomes normal to them. I believed that it was normal for me to be in prison, with brief periods of freedom sprinkled in. For me to feel that way, I had to be mentally ill. Unfortunately, there are no programs that de-program inmates from prison life. Some states have work release programs, re-entry programs, etc., but oftentimes inmates do not qualify for such a low-level security setting. I was able to go to a work release center but did not qualify to go off grounds unescorted.

Although my father clearly did not want me there, I felt he was my only hope. My father was a good man. One of his greatest strengths was that he always did the right thing, even if he knew there was a chance it would end up biting him in the ass. I was hoping to use that strength against him. I was hoping that if he looked me in the eyes, he'd do the right thing. All I had to do was get him to look me in the eyes.

The PA system crackled, and my bus was called. Oklahoma City to San Bernardino was about thirty-six hours and would give me some time to figure out what I would say to my father. I decided to be honest with him about everything, except for how this all began back in 1980. I settled into my seat in the back of the bus. I learned in prison to always keep my back to the wall in case someone tried to attack me. I closed my eyes so no one would try to initiate conversation with me and went back to the beginning.

CHAPTER 2

June 1980

I was nineteen years old and shared an apartment with my nineteen-year-old girlfriend. I worked as a delivery driver for a truck body shop, and my girlfriend worked at a pretzel shop in the local mall, in El Cajon, California. We went to work every day, and maybe drank a few beers or smoked a little weed on the weekends, but no narcotics.

One day, my girlfriend called me at work to tell me that her boss had accused her of stealing $20 from the register, which was not true. He had fired her and refused to release her final paycheck. Being nineteen years old, I made the (bad) decision to go confront her boss. I got into my vehicle and headed to the mall, my testosterone levels spiking.

I went directly to the pretzel shop and began verbally threatening her boss. He would not come out from behind the counter so I told my girlfriend we should go fuck up his car, and we headed to the parking lot. He followed us out, at a safe distance, and stood in front of his car. We made a few passes by him with my 1976 Chevy Blazer, shouting obscenities and threats at him as we passed. Someone shouted that they were going to call the police, so we decided to go home. No one was injured, and no property was damaged.

The next day, the El Cajon Police showed up at my apartment with a warrant for my arrest, for Assault with a Deadly Weapon. In California, the legal definition of assault is "intent" to do bodily injury, and the deadly weapon was my vehicle. The "victim" telling the police that he felt his life was in danger, combined with the threats I had shouted, was enough to charge me with the offense. I was handcuffed and transported to the San Diego County Jail, where I was booked, and bond was set at $10,000. I needed $1,000 to get out, and my girlfriend had promised to get me out as soon as she could.

The San Diego County Jail classifies inmates based upon the crime for which they are currently in jail. My charge was Assault with a Deadly Weapon, so I was housed in high security with other violent criminals: murderers, rapists, armed robbers, and gangbangers. I was nineteen years old, 6'2" 160 lbs., with long, curly blond hair. As soon as I stepped into the cellblock, I was greeted with men screaming, "FRESH MEAT!" I had never been so scared in my life.

I was assigned to a four-man cell with three Latino men. They were all gang members and were covered with tattoos, even on their faces. It was already time for lockdown when I got there, so I was hustled into the cell. No one said anything to me until the lights went out a few minutes later. Once the lights were out, the man with the "13" tattooed on his face told me to take off my clothes. I told him I'd rather not, and he laughed at me. He then showed me a shank, or homemade knife, and said, "You're either gonna get blood on my knife or shit on my dick, esse." The other two men grabbed me while "13" pummeled my face with punches. I started to scream, but one of them stuffed a sock in my mouth. A mattress was thrown onto the floor, my jail pants and underwear were taken off me, and I was forced, face down, onto the mattress. My face was forced into the mattress to muffle my screams. I remember wishing that I would suffocate to death, or at least pass out.

The actual rape only lasted about two minutes, but it felt like hours. Luckily, "13" was the only one who wanted to rape me, and to be honest, the other two looked a little disgusted by what they had participated in. "13" told me that if I snitched him off, or EVER told anyone, he would do the same thing to my family members, except that he would kill them afterward. I had absolutely no reason not to believe him, plus, I could never tell anyone that I had been raped by a man, so I never said a word to anyone about it, until shortly before I proposed to my current wife in 2016. I wanted her to know everything about me before she made a lifelong commitment to me.

The guards unlocked the cellblock for breakfast around 4:30 a.m., and I was told by "13" to take a shower. He handed me a bar of soap and a shampoo bottle. He told me to use the shampoo bottle, and its contents, as a douche to clean myself with. Everybody else in the cellblock knew what had happened the night before, and they were laughing at me. I was humiliated beyond humiliation. I showered and dressed, then sat in the dayroom, wrapped in a blanket.

At 8:30 a.m., my name was called for release. My girlfriend had raised the bail money. "13" reminded me of what would happen if I snitched and slapped me in the face for good measure. The Escort Officer took one look at my face and asked me what had happened. I told him that I fell in the shower, and he asked, "How many times?" I begged him to please just let me go home, to which he responded, "Don't come back."

That night, at home, I crawled into bed and fell asleep. Because I had stayed awake all night in jail, sleep came easily. My dreams, however, from that point on, were horrific. I dreamed that demons were raping and eating my girlfriend and my family members while I was forced to watch. My dreams were very graphic, and I remembered them vividly when I woke up. I woke up screaming, sweating, and crying every time I went to sleep. I contemplated suicide to make the nightmares end.

I knew some guys that used methamphetamine back then, and they would brag about being able to stay awake for days at a time, so I figured I'd try some before I resorted to suicide. The guy I bought the meth from was an intravenous drug user, and he convinced me that the meth would be much more effective if I shot up also. I said okay, and he shot me up with a quarter gram of some ether-based Peanut Butter Crank. The best meth in Southern California.

The "rush" was immediate and intense. The dopamine was coursing through my brain, and I had to check my crotch to see if I had ejaculated. The rush could only be compared to the intensity of an orgasm, and it lasted about thirty minutes. When the rush wore off, I was left with a feeling of elation. I felt like a kid in a candy store who was buying candy to take to Disneyland. I felt like I could do anything, except sleep and eat, neither of which I did for the next five days. When I finally crashed, I slept like the dead for eighteen hours straight, got up to use the restroom, then went back to sleep for another eight hours. I slept so deeply that I did not remember any of my dreams. I believed that I had found the solution to my nightmares, but I was actually about to make my newfound mental illness much worse.

Of all the criminal charges I've faced over the years, the only case I ever took all the way to trial was this *Assault with a Deadly Weapon* case. The rest were all settled via plea bargain. I was eventually found Not Guilty of *Assault with a Deadly Weapon*, but Guilty of *Disorderly Conduct*, a misdemeanor. I was sent to high security and raped over a misdemeanor.

CHAPTER 3

July 1980 – January 1982

Shortly after my newfound addiction began, I was scheduled to make a parts run from San Diego County to Los Angeles County for work. The day before the run, one of the supervisors at work noticed that I was acting strangely, and possibly displaying signs of being under the influence. I was asked if I had been drinking alcohol, and I said no. I was asked if I would be willing to take a urine test, and I agreed. I thought they were only testing me for alcohol, and I had not been drinking. Boy, was I wrong; I tested positive for methamphetamine, THC, and alcohol (from the night before). I was terminated on the spot.

I needed money, not only for drugs, but also for rent, utilities, food, etc., but instead of looking for another job, I decided I would sell meth. I had met several other meth-heads over the past few weeks, and they were always looking for quarter-grams, half-grams, and grams. I knew that if I could buy enough, the price would go down for me and maximize my profits. I needed about $1,000, but I only had $18.35. First, I tried borrowing money from friends and family, but when they all said no, I resorted to stealing from them instead. One of the worst things I ever did was steal Christmas from my family. On December 23, 1980, I broke into my family's house and stole all the Christmas presents under the Christmas Tree. It was a terrible thing to do, and I am ashamed to admit this story. I was subsequently arrested for this, and while I was in jail, my girlfriend broke up with me and moved all her belongings out of our apartment. The rent was already overdue, and by the time I was released from jail a few days later, I was homeless.

I couch-surfed between the few people who had not disowned me yet, but it wasn't long before I was unwelcome everywhere. One day I noticed a car left running outside a convenience store, so I hopped in and took off. I drove several miles away and parked in a strip mall parking lot, trying to figure out what to do next. I saw a few women carrying purses and calculated that I could grab someone's purse and make it back to my stolen car without any violence, and I was successful. People got my license plate number, but I didn't care – the car was stolen. Here I was, twenty years old, and I had just committed a strong-arm robbery. Big-time felony.

I made it as far as Las Cruces, New Mexico, where I was involved in a high-speed chase after I fled from a traffic stop. I was arrested after I flipped the stolen 280 ZX and was taken to the Dona Ana County Jail. New Mexico agreed to dismiss my charges if I waived extradition to California to face an assortment of felony theft and forgery charges, as well as strong-arm robbery. I waived extradition and was transported to the San Diego County Jail. The County Marshall who extradited me was a nice man, and I told him that I'd had problems in the jail before, but I was not specific. When we got to the jail, he asked the Intake Deputy if he could house me in a non-violent cellblock, even though I had a violent charge. Because of all the meth I was doing, I only weighed 140 lbs. At 6'2" tall, I was rail-thin, and did not look dangerous, so the Intake Deputy agreed.

After several months of going to court, I finally pleaded guilty to grand theft from a person (the purse snatching) and 2nd degree burglary (stealing Christmas from my family). As part of the plea agreement, I was sentenced as an adult, but incarcerated as a youthful offender. I was sentenced to three years and eight months in the California Youth Authority and was released on parole in January 1982. I had been incarcerated for just under one year from the day I was arrested. My time was easy to serve and I had no problems. Well, I did have one problem: I couldn't wait to shoot some meth.

CHAPTER 4

January 1982 – November 1984

My parents allowed me to live with them, along with my older brother, younger brother, and little sister. My parents purchased a vehicle for me, on which I would make monthly payments directly to them, interest-free. My dad, who worked for a uniform supply company, was able to talk one of his customers into hiring me as a delivery driver, delivering medical equipment and medical supplies to people's houses. Things went well for about one month, until I was offered some meth. I accepted and wound up not coming home for three days while I stayed in a motel room, shooting meth and partying with a woman I had met in a bar. When I finally went home, my parents asked me to move out, which I did.

I moved in with the woman I had met in the bar, and about one month later I was terminated from my job for stealing money from a customer's house while changing out their oxygen tanks. I had stopped making car payments to my parents, so they came and repossessed the car while I was asleep at home. The woman with whom I was living got tired of supporting me, and in September 1982, she kicked me out. I put all my belongings into a duffle bag and started walking. Not five minutes later, I came upon a vehicle parked in front of someone's house with its engine running. I hopped in and took off. After fleeing the scene, I opened the glove box and found a wallet containing $200 and several credit cards. I had never used a credit card before, but I had seen it done and felt confident that I could use a credit card to rent a motel room. I rented the room with no problems, but the next day I was awakened by the El Cajon Police Department (again) and arrested for auto theft and unauthorized use of a credit card.

I pleaded guilty to both charges in exchange for a one year sentence in the San Diego County Jail. I was sent to an "Honor Camp" in the mountains to serve my sentence. In February 1983, I escaped from the Honor Camp, and was arrested five days later in another stolen vehicle, with more stolen credit cards. I was sent to the California Institute for Men, in Chino, California, for a "90-day observation" to see if I was "prison material." I was returned to the San Diego County Jail twenty-one days later with a recommendation for probation. I hadn't even spoken with a case manager. I had only filled out paperwork and questionnaires. Oh well, cool with me.

The next day I was granted probation, on the condition I complete a one-year residential drug program. I agreed but knew I would not stay there long. The next day I was released to the custody of the drug program where I ate one meal, then snuck out the back door. I was on the lam again, but not for long. Three weeks later, I was arrested for using a stolen credit card as well as a probation violation.

Going in front of the same judge that sentenced me to probation was not a joyful reunion. He was livid. He told me he was disappointed that he could only sentence me to three years and eight months, but he still wanted to offer me help, so he sentenced me to three years and eight months in the California Rehabilitation Center (CRC), in Norco, California. CRC was a California Department of Corrections (CDC) prison which offered drug treatment to drug offenders. I was there for twelve months but never attended a single drug treatment class.

CRC was a Level 2 facility, with Level 1 being minimum-security, and Level 5 being Super-Max. CRC had gun towers, a double fence with razor wire and barbed wire on, and between, the fences. It was a real prison, but with dormitory-style barracks – 35 housing units with 100+ inmates per housing unit. That's over 3,500 men. We outnumbered the guards by at least 100 to 1, and the case managers by 200 to 1. Everyone was treated the same, with no specialized attention to anyone. I didn't learn anything that would keep me out of prison, but I did learn how to be more successful at committing crimes by listening to other people's stories.

I began lifting weights and grew into my 6'2" frame quickly. After only three months, I weighed 225 lbs., and I was bench-pressing 315 lbs. I picked a few fights that I knew I could win and established some credibility. Before long, I was accepted by a white supremacist group, who tattooed WHITE PRIDE on my triceps. I was treated with respect and fear, and began to feel that this was where I belonged.

It was while serving this sentence that my mental illness really progressed. Instead of learning a trade or attending Narcotics Anonymous (N.A.) meetings, I learned things like: how to light a cigarette with 2 AA batteries; how to beat a urine test; how to tie magazines around my body, underneath my shirt, to protect against being stabbed; how to fight dirty; how to hate other races; how to hate authority. A man must survive in prison, and only the strong survive. Trying to better oneself in prison is generally looked upon as being weak, as is attending religious services (unless one is Muslim, then it's ok).

I served my sentence like a man and departed with a good reputation. A couple of guys asked me to make phone calls for them after I got out, which I did. The calls were about smuggling drugs into CRC, but since the phones in prison are monitored, they didn't want to make the calls from inside. If I ever went back to prison, I would have furthered my reputation as a "stand-up dude" by keeping my word. I was released from CRC on parole on my 24th birthday.

CHAPTER 5

November 1, 1984 – June 1, 1985

The officer in Receiving & Release (R&R) filled out my release forms and asked me for my date of birth. I said, "November 1st, 1960." He said, "Well, happy birthday, young man. This is one birthday present you don't want to return." I told him I would not be back. It wasn't a lie…I never went back to that particular facility. When he asked for a forwarding address, I gave him my parents address in Santee, California (San Diego County). My parents had agreed to let me live with them until I "got on my feet." I was driven to the Greyhound station in Riverside where I boarded a bus to San Diego. Two hours later, my new life began.

My two brothers had moved out, but my little sister, only sixteen years old, still lived with my parents. They had a two-bedroom house, so I slept on a fold-out couch. My parents set house rules, which I did not like, but to which I agreed. I was twenty-four years old, and I had a curfew. After finding a job, I was to turn my paychecks over to my mother so she could show me how to budget my money, and to make sure I was saving money for a car and, eventually, to move out. I was assigned chores. At the first sign of drug usage, I would be asked to leave. It seemed there were more rules, stricter rules, there than in prison. I was pretty sure I'd figure out a shortcut or some way to speed up the process. Another life-tool I learned in prison.

I found a job with a construction company, and after four weeks, I was able to buy a car for $400. I stayed away from drugs for about two months. Someone at work offered me a shot of meth and I said "yes." After not coming home or calling for three days, my parents knew I was on meth again, and when I came home, my belongings were packed and sitting by the front door. I didn't even try arguing. I told them I was sorry and left.

I moved in with a couple of guys from work who had an apartment in Pacific Beach (San Diego), who only used drugs recreationally once in a while. I began to shoot meth every day, and it wasn't long before I lost my job. I had learned how to steal wallets from health club lockers while in CRC, as well as how to use a credit card, so I got to work. I purchased a set of 13" bolt cutters and a gym bag, put the bolt cutters in the bag with some sweatpants and a towel, and went into health club locker rooms. Once inside the locker room, I would look for an empty section and start cutting locks. I would cut about two or three locks, take the wallets, and leave. I would drive to the nearest mall and use the credit cards from the stolen wallets to purchase jewelry, electronics, clothing, etc. I would ask my drug dealers for orders in advance and would charge them 50% of whatever the receipt said.

My very first attempt was quite successful. I stole two wallets: one of them had $1,300 cash and six credit cards. The other, only $20 and no credit cards. I went directly to the mall and purchased a diamond wedding ring for $4,800 with one of the credit cards, and a whole new wardrobe for myself. I sold the ring for one ounce of meth, worth about $800 at that time. It wasn't 50% of what I paid, but an ounce of meth was more than I had ever had at one time, and just having a whole ounce made me feel like a kingpin. I had made $1,300 cash, plus $800 worth of meth, plus $600 worth of new clothing in less than two hours. I decided that day to become a career criminal.

I began going to the health clubs in San Diego County to steal wallets. At some health clubs, I would purchase a one-day membership for five or ten dollars just to get in. At others, I was able to waltz right in like I belonged there. I wasn't too worried about surveillance cameras back then. Cameras were few and far between, and the quality of resolution was poor. Besides, there was no facial-recognition software, so even if I was on video, nobody knew who I was. Whenever I got caught, however, there would be plenty of video evidence once they had me as a suspect. I didn't live my life thinking about the future back then, so I did nothing to cover my tracks. I had stopped going to my parole office visits after I started using drugs, and in January 1985, a warrant was issued for my arrest for "Absconding from Parole."

I began using more and more meth as my tolerance built. I was shooting a quarter gram or more at a time and shooting up at least ten times per day (I had become a pro with a syringe and was able to give myself shots with ease). I would stay awake for 6, 7, 8, 9, 10 days at a time without sleep, and very little food. When I was released from prison in November, I weighed 225 lbs. By January I was down to 180 lbs. By March I only weighed 145 lbs. The more weight I lost, the more I looked like a drug addict. The more drugs I consumed, and the more crimes I committed, the more paranoid I became. It was becoming harder and harder to successfully complete my crimes. I thought that every white car I saw was an unmarked police car following me. Some motel clerks would not rent rooms to me because I looked dangerous. In May 1985, one of my dealers got busted, and I was afraid he would tell the cops where all the expensive items he had came from me. I decided to leave California, so I hopped on a Greyhound and headed to Hicksville, New York, where I was born and raised until the age of 17.

I looked up old friends from my teenage years and received warm welcomes. I asked around to see if anyone knew where to score any meth. Meth was not popular in New York back then, but cocaine was everywhere. I had never used cocaine before, but I'd heard good things. I bought an 8-ball (3.5 grams) of coke and shot a quarter gram the first time, like I usually did with meth, but it was too much. My heart began to pound much harder than it did with meth and I began sweating profusely. Then came "the train." Anyone who has ever shot up cocaine knows what "the train" is. Imagine you are in a train tunnel and 2 or 3 trains come by at the same time, hauling ass and blowing their whistles. That's "the train." I lost the ability to hear anything at all, except "the train." I lost my balance and fell on the floor of the bathroom, the syringe still in my arm. I was sure I was going to die, which increased my heartbeat even more, but after about five minutes, my heart rate decreased, and my respiration slowed. I was going to live. You would think the valuable lesson learned here would be to stop using drugs before I overdosed and died. Due to my ever-intensifying mental illness, however, the only thing I learned was to do a little less the next time I shot cocaine…which was about thirty minutes later.

Cocaine differs from meth in one major feature: the length of the high. Meth has an initial rush that lasts 15 – 30 minutes, and a high that lasts several hours before the craving for more begins. Cocaine has an initial rush that lasts about ten minutes, and a high that lasts only fifteen minutes before the craving kicks in. I sat in a motel room by myself shooting coke all night long. By morning I felt terrible. The coke was gone, but I couldn't sleep due to all the coke in my system. It was a much harder come down than meth, but I finally slept.

CHAPTER 6

June 1985 – September 1985

I stole a 1978 Pontiac Trans Am in New York and started making my way south to Florida, stealing wallets from health clubs along the way. After arriving in Daytona Beach, I parked my stolen vehicle in the long-term parking at the airport and set out to look for another vehicle to steal. Cars were easy for me to steal now, because I would get the keys from the health club lockers along with the wallets, then go to the parking lot and use the keys to find the cars.

I used the Yellow Pages to find a health club and paid $5 for a 1-day membership. I went to the locker room, which I thought was empty, and started cutting a lock. Just then, an employee who had been using the restroom walked by and saw what I was doing. The bolt cutters were in my hand. I was busted. The employee did not try to physically restrain me, and I was able to leave, but I did not have a vehicle. I had to try to walk back to my motel room, which was about a half mile away, without being seen by a cop. I made it about a quarter mile when a police officer saw me. He was on his way to the health club to take the report, and he had my description. He stopped, detained me, and took me back to the health club to see if I could be identified by the witness. The witness positively identified me, and I was arrested.

Since I had an active warrant for violating my parole in California, I gave the police someone else's name and date of birth. That person was my younger brother, Chris. This was only the first time I used my brother's name. I would go on to use his name two more times, creating a criminal record for my unsuspecting brother. I was a monster. I was in the Volusia County Jail for 100 days when I pleaded guilty to attempted burglary of a structure, a misdemeanor, and was sentenced to 100 days in the county jail, with credit for 100 days of time served. I was released later that day with nothing at all. All my belongings were in my motel room, but that was 100 days prior, and everything was lost. I had no money, no clothes, no ID, and no place to stay. I did, however, still have the keys to the stolen Trans Am I parked at the airport. I walked to the airport, and to my surprise, the car was still there. It was going to cost over $100 to get the car out of the parking lot, but I had some old stolen credit cards, a gym bag, and bolt cutters in the car. I used one of the cards to pay the bill and drove to Miami.

I got into a health club without having to pay and went to the locker room. I went to an empty section and cut off a lock. Inside the locker was a backpack, and nothing else, so I took the whole backpack and crammed it into my gym bag. After driving to a safe location, I looked inside the backpack, hoping to find a wallet. Not only did I find a wallet, but also $2,000 in cash, a Rolex watch, a bag of cocaine, and a scale. I weighed the cocaine, and it came to 14 grams. I went to the Marriott Hotel and got myself a suite, where I spent the night shooting coke in the hot tub in my room. After consuming about 5 grams of the coke in about three hours, I heard a noise outside the door. I was sure it was the police, so I flushed the rest of the cocaine down the toilet. There were no cops, just my paranoia. It probably saved me from overdosing though, since I wouldn't have stopped until the dope was gone. I was done with cocaine. I had to find some meth, but the only place I knew I could find some for sure was in San Diego. I drove the Trans Am the airport, left it in the long-term parking lot, and bought a plane ticket to San Diego (it was pre-911, and I was able to use my court paperwork for identification to board the plane).

I landed in San Diego and took a cab to my dealer's house, where I bought some meth. I had been gone for several months, and he had lots of orders for me for merchandise. He drove me to a health club, where I stole a wallet and a car, and he followed me to the nearest mall, where I was able to purchase about $6,000 worth of merchandise that my dealer wanted. We went back to his house, where he gave me 2 ounces of meth for the merchandise. I drove my stolen car to a motel, got a room, and shot meth all night. What a life.

I picked up where I left off in the San Diego area, stealing wallets, running credit cards, living from motel to motel, having one-night-stands with random women, and stealing cars. One day I went to a health club in Bonita, California that I had never been to before. I paid $10 for a one-day pass and went to the locker room. Once inside, I randomly picked a locker and cut the lock off. I located the pants hanging from a hook inside the locker and attempted to remove the wallet. The wallet was too big and bulky, so I simply took the pants. I was hoping the wallet was big and bulky because it contained a large amount of cash and several credit cards. I drove a safe distance away and removed the wallet. The first thing I saw was a badge attached to the outside of the wallet. I opened the wallet, which turned out to not be a wallet, and saw official FBI credentials. I had just stolen an FBI agent's badge and credentials (OOPS!). No cash, no credit cards. Damn.

I knew it would be risky to try to sell this ID. If someone got caught with it, they would surely snitch me off. I had just met a woman, however, who got her meth from a biker gang, and I figured: if you can't trust a biker, who can you trust? I asked the woman if she thought the bikers might be interested in buying the badge and credentials. She called and asked them if they would be interested, and they said hell, yeah. Two bikers showed up thirty minutes later, examined the badge and credentials, and asked how I had acquired them. I told them about the locker room theft, but not specifically which health club, and they offered me one ounce of meth for both the badge and credentials, which

I accepted. I gave my lady friend a generous cut for facilitating the deal and left. I never saw her or the bikers again.

I went on my way, doing what I was doing like any normal day. Stealing and shooting meth had become normal to me. I would stay in motel rooms, all by myself, shooting dope and peeking out the windows. Sometimes I would burn tiny holes in the drapes so I could look outside. The more dope I shot, the more paranoid I became. I went days at a time without eating or sleeping. I began hallucinating on a regular basis, and even gave my paranoid hallucinations pronouns: "They/Them." Sometimes, I would drive for hours at a time because I believed that "They" were following me. Psychotic episodes became par for the course, and I accepted that those episodes were normal for me. I was drifting further and further into mental illness and did not have the ability to recognize it.

CHAPTER 7

October 1985 – January 1988

As I continued to steal wallets and shoot meth, I would sometimes fantasize about getting into a pro football or baseball team's locker room. On TV you could see that they don't even have doors on their lockers, much less locks. If I could only get into their locker rooms, I'd be rich. In November 1985 my fantasy came true.

I was driving around in the rain one day, very paranoid. I again believed that "They" were following me, and I was performing evasive maneuvers to lose my invisible followers. I got so paranoid that I parked my vehicle in an upscale residential neighborhood, just north of San Diego, got out and started running. I was scaling fences, running through yards, and getting very muddy. One female homeowner chased me out of her backyard, and as I reached her front yard, I slipped and fell in some mud. I was exhausted and was having trouble breathing. My heart was pounding. The homeowner stood over me yelling for me to get the hell out of there. I stood up and began to walk down the driveway.

The neighbor across the street was just backing out of his driveway and I asked him for a ride. He mistakenly thought that I lived across the street from him with the woman who was yelling at me, and he said ok. I got in and we drove away. We both saw police cars, apparently searching for me, and he asked if my wife might have called the cops on me. I said that she probably did, and begged him not to turn me in. He told me to recline my seat all the way back and to stay down. I was so exhausted from running, and being awake for days, that I fell asleep. He woke me up about an hour later. We were parked in the parking lot of the San Diego Sports Arena, and when I asked him what was going on, he told me that he played soccer for San Diego's professional soccer team, the San Diego Sockers, and was going in to practice. He suggested that I go in with him and watch the practice, then afterward he would take me to buy flowers for my wife and drive me home so we could make up. When we got to the door he told security that I was his guest, and I was in. What a nice man, so trusting. He was probably very sorry he ever met me when it was all over.

After seeing the team come out of the locker room several minutes later, I decided to make my move. I walked into the locker room and looked around. There were about twenty lockers, all full of personal items, and there were no doors on the lockers. Cha-Ching! I stole every wallet I could find, along with diamond rings, gold chains, and a Rolex Presidential watch. I also stole a set of car keys and left for the parking lot. The keys had VW emblems on them, and the first VW I tried the keys in worked. It was a brand-new Jetta with the sticker price tag still on the window. I took off and drove about twenty miles away where I rented a motel room and went through my haul. There was over $3,000 total cash and more credit cards than I would be able to use. I used one set of credit cards to buy more jewelry, at the request of one of my female dealers, and went to buy some meth from her.

I was still very excited about this score and told my dealer what had happened. She told me that I should get out of town for a while, and I agreed. She gave me an ounce of meth for the jewelry, and I left. I ditched the car in a country club parking lot and took a cab to the Greyhound station, where I boarded a bus to Las Vegas, Nevada.

Unbeknownst to me at the time, the woman who helped me sell the FBI agent's badge and credentials to the bikers got arrested for prostitution and made a deal with the police: let her go and she would tell them about a guy who stole an FBI agent's badge. She had just enough information for the police to verify that an FBI agent's badge and credentials had indeed been stolen from a health club locker, and that the date she gave them matched the date of the theft. The FBI sent an agent to talk to her and she told them everything she knew about me, including my real first and last name.

The FBI enlisted the help of the San Diego County Sheriff in order to find me. A detective was assigned, and an investigation began. A criminal background check was run on me, and my past was revealed. A quick computer check with surrounding agencies revealed more than 100 unsolved locker room thefts throughout San Diego County. Several warrants were issued for my arrest, including theft of government property, which was a federal charge. In November 1985 when the call came in for a locker room theft at the San Diego County Sports Arena, the case was sent to the detective assigned to find me. He showed an old jail booking photo of me to the neighbor who gave me a ride there, and he positively identified me. I became locally infamous overnight. My story was the lead story on all the local news channels that night. I was front page headline news in all the local newspapers the next day. I was labeled: Credit Card Dave, One Man Crimewave, and Meth Head by the local media outlets. They offered a reward for information leading to my capture. I was completely unaware any of this was going on.

When I started running low on meth I called my female dealer in San Diego to see if it was cool for me to come back, and she said NO WAY! She told me about the news stories, and I freaked out. I was already very paranoid, and this information made it exponentially worse. So, I did the normal thing, and shot some more dope. My female dealer friend agreed to bring some meth to me in Las Vegas since she was a little paranoid herself with all that was going on. We spent 3 days together in a motel room and said our good-byes. We both knew I would be caught soon and go to prison.

She had left me two of the newspaper articles about myself, which I put in my wallet along with a fake ID (that looked nothing like me). Two days later, I stole a rental car off a car rental lot. Five minutes later I was pulled over by the officer who was going to the car rental to take the stolen vehicle report. I gave the officer the fake ID, of which he was immediately dubious. He checked my wallet for any other identification and found the newspaper articles (with my picture on each). By this time several other officers had shown up, and when the arresting officer saw the newspaper articles, the date the articles were written, and my photos, he started bellowing with laughter. He told the other officers that I was carrying around my own arrest warrants. They passed the articles around, each one laughing at me and calling me America's Dumbest Criminal. I didn't argue. I had been awake for the past eleven days and was ready to go to jail. I was almost relieved that it was over. While being booked into jail, the nurse weighed me – 135 lbs. I looked like a skeleton shrink-wrapped in skin.

I was charged with auto theft in Nevada and "holds" were placed on me from the San Diego County Sheriff's Office for dozens of thefts and forgeries, as well as the Department of Justice for stealing the FBI agent's badge and credentials. I spent two months in the Las Vegas jail going to court and wound up pleading guilty to attempt/accessory to theft and was sentenced to thirty months in the Nevada Department of Corrections. After arriving at the prison, I used the prison law library to file an Interstate Agreement on Detainers (IAD) to force San Diego County to come get me from prison to face my charges in San Diego. After a couple of months, the detective who was working my cases in San Diego came to the prison where I was incarcerated with a writ of habeas corpus to extradite me to California.

I had been locked up for approximately ten months at this point, and for the past six months I had been working in the prison kitchen, eating very well and putting on lots of weight. I had also been lifting weights for the past six months and was very muscular. At this point, I weighed 245 lbs., and was 100 lbs. heavier than when I was committing most of my crimes. Prior to my arrest my hair was long and curly, but on this day, I was sporting a crewcut. The detective took one look at me and said I was not the prisoner he came to pick up. The lieutenant on duty told him I was the only David Joyce at that facility and to take me or leave me. The detective had a set of my fingerprints with him and asked the lieutenant for an ink pad and a piece of paper. After comparing my live fingerprints with the set he'd brought with him, he knew it was me. He said, "Boy, you've put on some weight." I responded with, "In fact, I've lost a few pounds. The food here sucks." I could see his hopes of multiple convictions fade away.

I was booked on over fifty felony charges of assorted thefts, credit card fraud, receiving stolen property, and forgery. I was looking at a significant amount of time in prison, but they had to convict me first. My appearance had changed so much that even a couple of my attorneys believed that I was innocent. I went to several line-ups, but no witnesses could identify me as the suspect. I wound up pleading guilty to one count of receiving stolen property and was sentenced to two years in prison, to run concurrently with my Nevada sentence of thirty months. I was returned to prison in Nevada, and one year later, still in Nevada State Prison, I was granted parole on my California sentence.

After returning from court in California, I filed a motion for the feds to come prosecute me for stealing the FBI agent's badge and credentials. Soon thereafter, I was extradited to the Metropolitan Correctional Center in San Diego to face my charge. Somewhere along the way, the badge and credentials had been recovered, and I was offered a 1-year sentence in a federal correctional facility if I pleaded guilty to misdemeanor theft of government property. I accepted the deal and was again returned to prison in Nevada. The judge allowed me to start my federal sentence while in state custody, but after discharging my Nevada sentence, I still owed the feds three months. The feds picked me up from prison, put me on "Con Air," which is nothing like the Nicholas Cage movie, and transported me to Federal Correctional Institute (FCI), Phoenix. I was released from federal custody with no parole, and no parole from Nevada, but I did owe California three years of parole. My parents agreed to let me stay with them in San Diego, so that's where I went. Only two years had passed since my arrest. I had learned another valuable prison lesson: how to beat the system.

CHAPTER 8

January 1988 – December 1994

The feds paid for my commercial flight from Phoenix to San Diego, but did not provide me with release money, so I was going to call my dad from the airport when I landed in San Diego and ask him to pick me up. On the plane, however, I met a man and struck up a conversation with him. I told him I had just been released from federal prison. This must have made him feel comfortable with me, because he told me he had an ounce of meth down his pants and asked me if I wanted to do some when we landed. He also told me he would pay for a motel room, buy me a change of clothes, give me some pocket money, and introduce me to some women he was meeting up with that night. I knew that if I did some dope, I would not make it to my parents' house, and they would be disappointed in me...again. I chose meth over my family...again.

After we landed, he was true to his word on all counts. A friend of his was waiting at the airport to pick us up and we drove to a motel room. My new friend paid for the room, and we went inside to do some dope. He was a snorter (people who snort their dope), and many snorters don't like slammers (people who use intravenously), so I snorted the meth he offered me. It had been over two years since I'd gotten high, and I got pretty high by snorting the meth, but I wanted to shoot up. He had to run some errands and left me alone in the motel room to shower and get ready to go to a club. As soon as he left, I walked to a local pharmacy and bought a box of 100 syringes. I went back to the motel room and did a shot of dope. Aaaahhhh, sweet euphoria. That first shot after being clean for so long was very satisfying. I knew I would be going back to my sleazy ways, but I did not care. This feeling was the only thing I cared about. I also chose this feeling over following the terms and conditions of my parole. I had seventy-two hours to report to the San Diego parole office, where I would undoubtedly be asked to provide a urine sample for drug testing. I knew from past experience that one positive drug test would probably not violate my parole, and I planned to take my chances.

My new friend took me to a club with him, where, true to his word, he introduced me to some women. One of the women and I hit it off pretty well and we went back to my motel room to do some meth. We wound up having sex and spending the night together. We agreed to see each other again, but no specific plans were made at the time. She gave me the phone number to her mother's house where she lived, and I promised to call soon.

I had already purchased a gym bag and bolt cutters, and there was a health club within walking distance from my motel, so I went to "work." I was able to steal three wallets and a set of car keys from the locker room. I found the car easily in the parking lot and drove to the nearest shopping mall. I had told my new friend about my credit card hustle, and he had given me a list of things he would buy from me. I was able to purchase over $6,000 worth of merchandise that my new friend wanted. I contacted him to let him know what I had purchased, and he came right over. I charged him $2,000 for the merchandise, and he gave me $1,000 in cash plus one ounce of meth. We were both happy.

I went to a salvage yard and bought a 1972 Cadillac El Dorado for $200. It needed a new starter, which I paid someone $50 to replace, and I was ready to go. I had no registration, no insurance, and no driver's license, but the car was not stolen and that was all I cared about. I picked up where I had left off two years prior, stealing wallets and shooting dope.

I never even called my family after my release, until I got arrested...
again. I tried to contact the woman I had spent the night with, but she
was rarely at home at her mother's house (cell phones were not around
then). I spent the next three weeks staying in motel rooms, stealing, and
getting high.

I had reported to the parole office three days after my release and
gave my parole officer a urine sample that I knew would test positive for
methamphetamines. The urine test kits had advanced in technology by
this time and my parole officer was able to test my urine on the spot. Of
course, I tested positive for meth. I told him that I had snorted a line
while celebrating my release, but promised it was a one-time thing. He
told me that I would have to submit to a urine test weekly, and if I tested
positive one more time, he would violate my parole and send me back
to prison. I decided to not report to the parole office anymore, and after
missing my appointment the next week, a warrant was issued for my
arrest, for absconding from parole.

Twenty-one days after my release, I was able to get in touch with the
woman I had spent the night with the night I was released. I gave her
the address of the motel I was staying in and she came over. I had just
bought some meth from someone I had recently met and when my lady
friend got there, we did some of the meth. Immediately we realized that
the meth was no good. Neither of us felt high afterward, so I called my
dealer and told him I wanted my money back. He told me to bring the
unused dope back to him and he would give me my money back. It was 2
a.m., but I hopped into my Cadillac anyway, and went to return the dope
while my lady friend waited in the motel room. I carelessly ran a red light
in front of a cop and was pulled over. I had no license, no registration,
and no insurance. I gave the cop my real name, hoping that a warrant
had not been issued for my parole violation yet. Unfortunately for me,
the warrant had been issued, and I was arrested. As per procedure, the
officer searched me and found the dope I was returning for a refund

because it was of low quality. Unfortunately for me again, the meth was good enough to test positive for methamphetamines, and I was charged with possession of a controlled substance and transported to the San Bernardino County Jail. I had only been out for twenty-one days.

The police found my motel key, which had the name and room number of the motel on the tag and got a search warrant to search my room. I had drug paraphernalia in the room (syringes), but nothing else illegal. The police informed my lady friend that I was going to jail, and they were impounding my vehicle. I didn't expect to hear from her ever again, but I was wrong.

A couple of days after my arrest, I was called for a visit. It was my lady friend. She promised to visit and write to me while I was in jail, which I greatly appreciated. After being in jail for one month, I told my lady friend that California had "conjugal visits" in prison, and that if we got married while I was in the county jail, we could get conjugal visits once I got to prison. She asked me if I was proposing to her, and I said yes, I was. She said ok, and we were married in the judge's chambers after my sentencing hearing. I had pleaded guilty to the possession charge and was sentenced to sixteen months in the California Department of Corrections. Two months later, I got my first conjugal visit in prison. It was great.

After serving ten months of my sentence, I was granted parole and moved into a travel trailer with my bride. She was a meth addict, and had access to some really good meth, so I wasted no time getting back to my "normal" lifestyle. I didn't even bother reporting to the parole office this time and began stealing immediately. After about three months of stealing and shooting dope, my wife and I had decided to leave the state and travel to New York, where I still had childhood friends. I rented a brand-new Cadillac with a stolen credit card, and we hit the road.

We got as far as Denver, Colorado when we ran out of meth. My wife called someone in San Diego, who agreed to send us an ounce of meth and an ounce of marijuana. The drugs were sent via Continental Airline's "Quick Pack" package delivery service. The person in San Diego packaged the dope in a shipping box and took it to the airport in San Diego where the package was put on the next Continental flight to Denver. We went to Stapleton Airport in Denver to pick up the package, but it did not go well.

Our package was deemed to be of a "suspicious nature" and was opened to inspect the contents prior to my wife picking up the package. The drugs were found by Continental Airline employees and the police were called. When my wife went into the airport to pick up the package, the Continental Airlines employee at the counter was actually an undercover police officer. He told my wife that the package had accidentally opened up coming out of the plane and he noticed there was some speed and some weed in the box. He told her that if she gave him five or ten bucks, he wouldn't say anything. She gave him $20, took the package, and left. I was waiting just outside the exit doors, and as soon as she reached me, she said, "Let's get the fuck out of here." Just then, we were surrounded by law enforcement officers, guns drawn, screaming at us to get on the ground. I had been free for about four months this time. Not bad.

My wife and I were arrested and booked into the Denver County Jail for two counts of conspiracy to import of a controlled substance. My wife was able to get a family member to post her bond and she returned to San Diego. I had a hold placed on me from California for parole violation, and I was not able to post bond. My wife was facing 12 to 24 years in prison for each count, and, since I was on parole at the time, I was facing 24 to 48 years in prison for each count. On top of this, the prosecutor filed the Habitual Criminal Act on me, which carried a sentence of forty years to life. Even though I never touched the drugs, I was charged with conspiracy to import. If they could prove that I knew about the package I would be spending the rest of my life in prison.

After spending eleven months in jail going to court hearings, I was offered a plea bargain. If I pleaded guilty to simple possession of a controlled substance, I would be sentenced to five years in the Colorado Department of Corrections, with credit for the eleven months I had already served. If I pleaded guilty, my wife would receive probation. If not, my wife would go to prison. I pleaded guilty and took my five years like a man. My wife was sentenced to five years of probation and was allowed to serve her probation in San Diego. She visited me in the jail that night and promised to come visit me in prison, as well as to send me money to live on while I was locked up. That was in March 1990. That was the last time I ever saw her. When I got to prison and realized that she had left me, I filed for divorce.

In December 1990, I was allowed to go to work release, where I got a job telemarketing for a long-distance phone company. After two years, I was granted parole and released from the work release center. I was only out for three weeks, when I was arrested for attempting to steal a wallet from a health club locker. I was convicted and sentenced to three years in the Colorado Department of Corrections. I was released on parole in September 1993, and discharged my parole nine months later. On June 1, 1994, the day I discharged my parole, I celebrated by doing a very generous helping of meth and returned to my old ways. I made it until December 1994 without being arrested...again.

CHAPTER 9

December 1994 – April 1997

I had heard that the state of Texas had recently changed their laws, and non-violent felonies carried a maximum sentence of two years in a state jail. State Jails are part of the Texas Department of Criminal Justice, but only house non-violent offenders serving sentences up to two years. By this time, I could do two years standing on my head, so I figured, why not?

I was only in Texas for one week and was arrested. My initial arrest was just outside of Ft. Worth, for theft and credit card fraud, and met my court appointed attorney at my second court hearing. My attorney informed me that Texas had recently elected a very liberal Democrat governor, and under the new laws passed since her inauguration, I was guaranteed probation for all my charges. I was ecstatic. I was sentenced to three years' probation for nine counts of theft and credit card fraud and was released. I was supposed to report directly to the Probation Department, but I decided not to. I knew I would be caught eventually, but by this point in my mental illness, my lifestyle had become normal to me. I was caught in a cycle that I could not break, but that was because I did not try.

I was able to contact a friend who lived in Oklahoma. He told me that he was cooking dope (manufacturing methamphetamine), and I should come to Oklahoma. He said he had a huge list of merchandise he wanted, and that he had plenty of meth and money. I went to Oklahoma and started stealing. I mainly stuck to the health clubs in Oklahoma

City and Tulsa and traveled back and forth between the two cities. I had purchased a 1976 Lincoln Continental, but never registered the vehicle in my name, and by May 1995, the old registration had expired.

On July 2, 1995, I was pulled over by a police officer in Midwest City, Oklahoma. I had just left my motel room with seven grams of meth and my syringe kit, after doing a shot of dope. It was very hot and humid that day, and I was wearing a long-sleeved shirt (to hide the needle marks on my arms), so I was sweating profusely. I was hoping that Texas had not yet issued a warrant for my arrest, but after the officer ran my name, he discovered that I was wanted in Texas for probation violation. When he asked me to step out of the vehicle, I put my car in DRIVE, and sped away.

My vehicle had a big 8-cylinder engine, and though it was twenty years old, it had some get-up-and-go left in it. The police officer's car, however, had much more get-up-and-go than my car. I kept driving, even though I was pretty sure I wasn't going to get away. It was a Sunday afternoon, and traffic was moderate. Adrenaline was coursing through my body, and I had been high on meth for eight days at this point. My vehicle had no air conditioning, and I had no water with me. I was dehydrating very rapidly. I was in panic mode. The longer I drove, the more police cars joined the chase. About fifteen minutes into the pursuit, I saw two helicopters above me. After a full hour of being chased, I was running low on gas, and I knew I would be caught soon. I knew the most serious crime I would be arrested for would be the meth, so I tried to figure out how to get rid of it. I considered opening the baggie of dope and eating it, but seven grams of meth would probably kill me, so I decided to try to get back to my motel room in Oklahoma City and flush the dope down the toilet.

As I was approaching the motel, I noticed the police had backed off slightly, probably wanting me to drive slower as well. I pulled into the parking lot of the motel, stopped in front of my room, and got out of my car. I ran to the room, put my key in the door, and made it inside. I slammed the door shut and wedged a chair under the doorknob. I heard the police yelling for someone to get the key from the front desk, so I figured I had time to get rid of the dope by flushing it down the toilet. Just then, the landline telephone in my room started ringing, and I had assumed it was the police. This made me realize that they were going to try to talk me out of the room, and I would probably have time to do a shot of dope before they kicked in the door.

I usually shot up about one quarter of a gram of meth at a time, but due to my situation, I decided to double my portion. I fixed a half-gram shot, stuck the needle in my arm, and blasted off. The rush was intense, and my ears started ringing. After a few minutes I heard the phone ringing, and I answered it. It was a police lieutenant with the Oklahoma City Police Department. The room was rented in my real name, and the lieutenant addressed me by David. He informed me that the motel was completely surrounded, and that I should come out. I asked him if smoking cigarettes was permitted in the jail I was going to, and he said no. I told him I would come out after I finished all of my cigarettes, and he asked how many cigarettes I had left. I said I had five cartons and hung up on him.

I heard a noise by the window of my room, and thought the cops were going to come in through the window, but the noise stopped. I peeked through the curtains and saw that the window was now covered by a blanket. I looked through the peephole in the door and saw it was also covered up. They did not want me looking outside. Then I heard helicopters flying overhead and assumed that one of the helicopters was a news helicopter, and this situation might be broadcast live. I turned on the TV, flipped through a few channels, and found it. I was able to watch the police in the parking lot on TV and would be able to see when they were about to force entry into my room.

A negotiator kept calling my room, attempting to coax me out and surrender. I kept stalling by telling them I would kill myself if they came in the room. Meanwhile, I was watching them on TV and casually doing shot after shot of meth. After four hours of patiently waiting me out, I saw the officers putting on extra gear and picking up riot shields. I knew they were coming in soon, so I flushed the remaining two grams, or so, of meth down the toilet. I had drug paraphernalia and bolt cutters, but those would not result in any serious felony charges. I watched the police coming toward the room with their guns drawn and I stood in the middle of the room with my hands raised toward the ceiling. The police broke the window of the motel room and ordered me to get on the ground. I complied with all of their commands and was taken into custody and transported to the Oklahoma County Jail. I was charged with dozens of driving offenses, as well as resisting arrest, and a hold was placed on me from Texas for probation violation.

I went to court a few days later and my court appointed attorney told me that if I signed extradition to Texas, Oklahoma would dismiss all of my charges stemming from the car chase and standoff. I agreed and five days later, I was extradited to Texas. I was sentenced to two years in a state jail and released in April 1997. Needless to say, I had not learned any valuable lessons from this ordeal. In fact, I needed to be locked up for a while. The day I was arrested in Oklahoma City, I weighed 140 lbs., and the day I was released, I weighed 245 lbs. I'd received many breaks along the way, with relatively short sentences, and I began looking at my incarcerations as occupational hazards, as well as recuperations from my drug usage. In July 1997, my breaks ran out.

CHAPTER 10

April 1997 – July 1997

During the time I was incarcerated in Texas, I had no contact with anyone from the outside world. I received no visits and no mail. None of the people I had been associating with had landline phones to accept collect calls, so I spoke with no one on the outside. I was released on April 4, 1997, and called my parents from a pay phone to ask if I could come stay with them. They said ok, and even sent me money via Western Union for a bus ticket to San Diego and for food along the way. My parents had come through again.

While waiting for the bus, I used a pay phone to call my old dealer's pager. A minute later, the pay phone rang, and it was my old dealer. I told him I had just been released from prison in Texas and was waiting for a bus to San Diego. He told me that while I was locked up, he had been arrested by the DEA for trafficking methamphetamine. He was out on bond, awaiting sentencing, and was expecting to receive an 8-year sentence in federal prison. He was no longer involved with meth, was unemployed, and needed money to feed his family. He asked me to come to Oklahoma City and help him financially by stealing wallets. He said he would drive me wherever I needed to go and be my getaway driver. I told him I did not want to disappoint my parents again and that I was definitely going to California. He asked me to come to OKC first, make some money, then go to my parent's house. I didn't want to be too much of a burden to my family, and figured I would at least be able to buy some clothes, so I agreed.

I traded my bus ticket to San Diego for a ticket to OKC instead, where my friend picked me up at the Greyhound station. He had with him a gym bag, a set of bolt cutters, and the Yellow Pages. We found the nearest health club and drove to it. I paid $5 for a one-day guest pass and went inside. I picked a locker at random and cut the lock off. I grabbed the wallet and looked inside. It was a very thick wallet and I saw plenty of credit cards and cash. I left the health club and hopped into my friend's car. I told him to drive to the nearest shopping mall while I went through the wallet. I first went to the billfold section to count the cash and discovered thirty-five 100-dollar bills (my largest cash theft ever). There were also several credit cards, with which I purchased a total of $8,000 worth of merchandise, including new clothes for myself. I kept a few of the purchased items to sell later and gave my friend approximately $7,000 worth of merchandise for him to sell, along with $500 cash. He dropped me off at a hotel (The Marriott), where I booked a flight from OKC to San Diego for the next morning (this was pre-911, when I was still allowed to fly). My friend took me to the airport the next morning, and I headed to my parent's house.

My original plan was to find a job and stay away from the drugs, but after being so successful in my very first endeavor after being released from prison, I had decided to only visit with my parents for a few days, then go back to Oklahoma and go back to stealing and shooting meth. I told my parents that an old friend in Oklahoma was getting ready to go to federal prison and asked me to live in his house, and take care of it, until he got out. I also told my parents that my friend was able to get me a job working on an oil rig, and that he had paid me $3,000 he owed me from 1995. My parents were very happy for me, and our week-long visit was very enjoyable. I purchased a 1978 Lincoln Continental for $1,800 while I was staying with my parents. I left my parent's house on good terms for once and headed back to Oklahoma. That was the last time I saw my mother.

My friend in Oklahoma refused to cook any dope for me, but he did introduce me to some people who sold meth, and I became a regular customer. I stole wallets and shot meth every day, sleeping once or twice a week. I had met a woman along the way who was enamored with my lifestyle and wanted to be with me. I told her I would eventually get caught and go to prison, and if she was with me, she would probably be arrested as well. She told me she was on probation but had not reported to the Probation Department in several weeks and was probably wanted for probation violation in Missouri. I said ok, and we traveled around the surrounding states, stealing wallets and shooting meth, but always coming back to Oklahoma to buy more meth.

In July 1997, we drove to Bartlesville, Oklahoma to steal some wallets so I could get a credit card to purchase a 48" Sony TV (the kind that came on wheels). In the event I was successful, I had a friend in Bartlesville who owned a pickup truck on standby to pick the TV up from the store and drive it an hour away to Tulsa. I was successful. Inside the locker was $500 cash and two credit cards on a money clip. I stopped at a grocery store and purchased $500 worth of gift certificates with one of the credit cards so my girlfriend and I would be able to buy food, then went to the mall, where I purchased the 48" Sony with one of the credit cards. After completing the purchase, I told the clerk I would be back in a few minutes with a pickup truck to get the TV and left the store. We drove to my friend's house a few minutes away, shot some meth with him, and went back to the mall to pick up the TV.

My girlfriend and my friend waited in their vehicles in the parking lot while I went inside the store to receive the TV I had purchased with the stolen credit card. When I got to the electronics department, I saw there was a Bartlesville Police Officer near the counter speaking with the salesperson who sold me the TV. As I got closer, the salesperson said to the officer, "There he is now." Apparently, they had realized that the credit card I used was not mine, and the officer asked me for identification. I

BREAKING THE CYCLE | DAVID JOYCE

said it was out in the car and that I would go get it. I left the store and ran to my girlfriend's vehicle, with the police officer not far behind. I got in the passenger seat and yelled, "GO! GO! GO!" while the officer was yelling, "STOP! STOP! STOP!" My girlfriend was frozen in fear until the officer reached inside the vehicle, and across her body, to grab the car keys. Just then she popped the clutch and sped off with the officer's arm still inside the car. The officer was able to pull his arm out of the car without being injured, but as we learned in Chapter 1, assault is the "intent" to do bodily harm; and a vehicle may be deemed a deadly weapon.

We got out of the parking lot and onto the main road, but we tried to get to some back streets and stay off the main roads. After about one minute, we were spotted by a police officer. When my girlfriend pulled over, I got out and ran. It was over 100 degrees outside, and I had been up shooting meth for four days without sleep or food. I ran for about 100 yards, then ran out of breath. I refused to follow the officer's commands to get on the ground and squared off to fight the officer. He pulled out a telescopic asp and hit me on the side of my knee. I dropped like a bag of cement and the officer handcuffed me. I was transported to the Washington County Jail and booked in on two counts of unauthorized use of a credit card, two counts of possession of a credit card belonging to another, and one count of theft. It looked like I would be going to prison for a couple of years...again.

CHAPTER 11

June 1997 – December 1997

After being booked into the jail, I was housed in a six-man cell with five other men and assigned a bunk. I climbed into the bed and went to sleep. A jailor woke me up the next morning to go to my arraignment. This hearing was held virtually, and I fell asleep waiting for my name to be called. A few minutes later the jailor was shaking me awake and telling me to stand up. I saw my girlfriend, in an orange jumpsuit, in the back of the room, and she was standing also. I was groggy and not paying attention to the judge, but to my girlfriend. As I turned my attention to the judge, I heard him say, "$500,000 cash or surety for both defendants." I thought, surely, that couldn't be our bond. We were escorted out of the makeshift courtroom and taken back to our cells. I asked the jailor how much our bonds were, and he said, "Half a million dollars each." I said, "For credit cards?" He said, "Welcome to Oklahoma."

When I got back to my six-man cell, I spoke to my cellmates for the first time. I asked how much time in prison unauthorized use of a credit card carried. They said two to seven years unless I had two or more prior convictions. Then the punishment would be twenty years to life. I then understood why our bonds were so high. My girlfriend was charged with assault on a police officer with a deadly weapon and was also facing twenty years to life. I was also told that the prosecutor was a real hard-ass, with vanity license plates on his personal vehicle that read, "FRY-EM." Not even "white privilege" was going to save me this time.

After four months of court hearings, I was offered a plea bargain. The State would dismiss the theft charge if I pleaded guilty to the four credit card charges and ask the judge to sentence me to twenty-five years in the Oklahoma Department of Corrections for each count, but for each count to be run concurrently. One hundred years crammed into one twenty-five year sentence. Keep in mind that the $500 cash was recovered and returned to the victim, as was the $500 worth of grocery gift cards. The 48" Sony TV had never left the store. Financially, no one lost a single penny. How was it possible that I was going to prison for twenty-five years? My attorney had advised me that if I decided to take my case to trial and was found guilty on all five charges, my sentences would likely run consecutively. I would be looking at twenty years minimum on each count, for a total of one hundred twenty years to life. I reluctantly accepted the plea bargain and returned to court for sentencing a few weeks later.

At the time of our arrest, all my belongings were in suitcases inside our vehicle. Inside the suitcases was a poem entitled, *Credit Card Dave*, and written by me. The poem was a boastful, rhyming account of my drug usage and life of crime, and "FRY-EM" (the prosecutor) planned to make this poem known to the judge at sentencing. Judges don't usually have mercy on cocky defendants, and I was no exception to the rule.

FRY-EM read my poem aloud in the courtroom as I tried to look ashamed of myself. Inside, however, I was very proud of myself. I even heard spectators in the audience laughing. My poem ended with me getting away with my crimes, and FRY-EM would not allow that to happen in real life. After reading my poem aloud, he said to the judge, "Your Honor, at this point in Mr. Joyce's life, I feel his poem is incomplete and that a few more stanzas should be added. Perhaps they should go like this..." and he recited a poem that he, himself, had written called, *An Ode to Dave*. It is now twenty-six years later, and though I do not remember every word of *Credit Card Dave*, I do remember every word of *An Ode to Dave*, as well as every word of my poetic response to his poem.

An Ode to Dave

Again, he stands before the court,
In shackles and in chains –
He wants us all to pity him,
For all his many pains.

But now it's time to answer,
For all the crime he's done –
At last, he finds out life is more,
Than simply having fun.
The message in his life,
Is truly crystal clear -
He thinks that he is clever,
And someone we should fear.
But in the end, I say to you,
A very old cliché:
Those that live a life like this,
Find out that crime doesn't pay.

I was completely dumbfounded, but also impressed. It was incomprehensible to me that a District Attorney had taken the time to write a poem about me. This was a non-violent property offense, where no one lost any money. The day after each of my court hearings, I was front page headline news in the Bartlesville Examiner-Enterprise, and the day after receiving my twenty-five year sentence was no exception. The headline read: PRISON TIME FOR CREDIT CARD DAVE, and *An Ode to Dave* was just below the headline. After reading the poem several times, I wrote a poem in direct response to FRY-EM's poem and sent it to the Bartlesville Examiner-Enterprise, which they declined to print. They did not want *Credit Card Dave* to have the last word. My poem was called, *An Ode to Curtis*.

An Ode to Curtis

Again, I stood before the court,
To pay for what I'd done –
There always is a price to pay,
When you think that stealing's fun.
I asked them not for pity,
But to understand my fears –
When the judge told me I was a waste,
My eyes then filled with tears.
I may think I am clever,
But to fear me would be silly –
It's not like I'm a killer,
Or a baby-raping hillbilly.
The sentence that was handed down,
Surely must be served –
Even though it was extreme,
And more than I deserved.
But the thing that I'll remember most,
Even more than his cliché –
Is the poetic justice I received,
And to him I say, touché.

In early December 1997, I was transported to the Lexington Assessment and Reception Center, in Lexington, OK to begin serving my twenty-five year sentence. If I played by the rules, I could be out in about eight more years. I did not play by the rules.

CHAPTER 12

December 1997 – October 2000

My sentence began at the super-maximum-security unit of the Lexington Assessment and Reception Center (LARC) in Lexington, Oklahoma. Everyone sentenced to state prison in Oklahoma begins their sentence at LARC. Inmates are checked for medical issues, tested for intelligence, and classified for security. I was thirty-seven years old and in good physical condition; I tested at the 12th grade level; and, surprisingly, I was classified minimum-security. The length of my sentence was not a factor in determining my security level, and since my crime was non-violent, as were my prior convictions, I was sent to the Jess Dunn Correctional Center in Taft, Oklahoma. Two days later I was assigned a job: picking up trash on highways. One minute later I began thinking about escaping.

I hung in there for nearly two years before I escaped. Our work crew consisted of eight inmates and one (unarmed) correctional officer. On September 9, 1999, we were helping the Oklahoma Department of Transportation (ODOT) replace a guardrail along a freeway in Tulsa. I happened to notice that someone had left the keys in the ignition of one of the ODOT pickup trucks, and, very impulsively, I got in the truck and drove off. I went directly to a health club and stole three wallets and a set of car keys with a remote access key fob. I went to the parking lot, located the car, and took off. I was wearing a pair of state issued blue jeans, a white T-shirt, a yellow reflective vest, and a ballcap that said ODOT on it. I looked like a highway worker. I drove to a local mall and used the credit cards to purchase new clothes, then drove directly to Kansas City, Missouri. I had gotten away, and I was exhilarated.

I had chosen the Kansas City area because I had seen a news program that named Independence, Missouri "The Methamphetamine Capital of the World," and I was ready to shoot some meth. I spent the first two days stealing and amassing items to trade for drugs, and the third day trying to find a dealer. I met a woman in a bar who looked like she was high on meth. We struck up a conversation and about fifteen minutes later I asked if she knew where I could buy some meth. She did not know where to get any meth, but she did know where to get some cocaine. I gave her $150, and she got me three grams of coke. The coke was very good, and it only took a little bit to get me high. I had been clean and sober for over two years, and that first shot was euphoric.

After getting high, I told the woman that I had jewelry, electronics, and department store gift cards for sale or trade. She introduced me to her dealer, who was very interested in trading coke for merchandise. He and I formed a "business relationship" and we both got what we wanted. Brand-new, untraceable, merchandise for him, unlimited cocaine and cash for me. He gave me "wish-lists" on a regular basis, and as I filled his orders, he paid me in coke and cash. Five months later, in February 2000, my luck ran out.

I was in a motel room in Overland Park, Kansas with a woman I had met. It was her motel room, rented in her name. Immediately after we shot up some coke, there was a knock on the door. I looked through the peephole and saw two police officers outside the door. I asked them what they wanted, and they said they needed to speak with the woman who rented the motel room. I was hoping I would be able to bullshit my way out of getting arrested, so I opened the door. The two officers went to my lady friend, told her they had a warrant for her arrest, then cuffed her. While the female officer was searching my friend, the male officer asked me for identification. After telling him I had no ID, I told him my name was Randy White and gave him a fictitious Social Security number and date of birth. After a records search the dispatcher notified the officer that there was no record matching the information I gave him. He knew I was lying about my name and told me that if I didn't give my real name, he would take me to jail and identify me through my fingerprints. I was going to jail either way, so I stuck with the name Randy White.

I was booked on the charge of suspicion of obstructing justice, then fingerprinted and photographed. I returned to the holding cell and fell asleep. I awoke to an officer calling for David Joyce, but I did not respond. The officer asked me for my name, and when I said Randy White, he asked me to come with him. My fingerprints had revealed my true identity, and the fact that I was wanted by the Oklahoma Department of Corrections for escape from custody. I was re-booked under David Joyce for felony obstruction of justice (for lying about my name), and a hold was placed on me from Oklahoma for the escape so I could not post bond. The obstruction charge carried a maximum penalty of eleven months in the Kansas Department of Corrections (KDOC), which I could not believe. Prison time for telling a lie? If telling a lie is a felony, why are politicians not arrested every time they open their mouths?

After sitting in the Johnson County Jail for six months, I decided to plead guilty to the obstruction charge and go finish the eleven month sentence in a Kansas prison. With good time, I had just over three months left to serve. No problem. David Joyce was sentenced to eleven months in the Kansas Department of Corrections, and transported to the KDOC reception center in Topeka, Kansas.

When I got to the reception center, I found out that all of my paperwork had the name Randy White on it. I informed the staff that my real name was David Joyce, and the name Randy White was the fake name I was in prison for using. I was told that they could not change the name on any paperwork that came from the courts. I was hoping this clerical error would work to my advantage. Boy, did it ever.

After ten days of medical testing, intelligence testing, and security classification, Randy White was classified minimum-security. Randy White did not have a hold from Oklahoma, nor did he have a criminal record. Randy White was transported to the minimum-security unit at the Lansing Correctional Facility in Lansing, Kansas, and eight days later, David Joyce escaped from prison...again.

Lansing is located approximately twenty-five miles from Kansas City, Missouri, which is where I needed to go. I was immediately assigned to a job mowing the grass outside the prison fences, and I used the opportunity to get a lay of the land. I noticed a railroad track and asked a fellow inmate where the tracks let to. North led to St. Joseph, Missouri, and south led to Kansas City, Kansas and Missouri. Kansas City was closer, and I knew people there, so I decided I would climb the sixteen foot fence of the facility on Saturday morning and follow the train tracks to Kansas City.

The sixteen foot fence was also equipped with barbed wire and razor wire but was stretched so tight that there were big gaps in the barbs and razors. I was dressed in blue jeans, a white T-shirt, a heavy denim coat, and a black beanie cap. I was also wearing thick gardening gloves to protect my hands. The inmates were regularly released for medication line after the 4 a.m. count cleared, usually around 4:30 a.m., and on Saturdays there were no additional security counts until 10:30 a.m. If I got away cleanly, I would have about six hours to make it to Kansas City. The count cleared at 4:25 and I went to the medication line to get my arthritis medication. After taking my meds, I walked behind the gymnasium where the fence was shorter than the building and looked around. No one would see me unless they walked behind the gymnasium, and at this time of day, no one would have a reason to do that. I took a deep breath and began climbing. I hadn't climbed a fence in decades, but my adrenaline was pumping, and I was determined to escape. I reached the top of the fence but got hung up on the razor wire while I was trying to get over the fence. After several minutes of struggling to free myself, I was able to use my body weight to free my clothing from the razor wire by letting go of the fence and twisting my body like a gator drowning its prey. I fell approximately ten feet to the ground, but I was on the outside, and that was all that mattered.

I headed for the railroad tracks while I assessed my clothing and possible injuries. My coat and pants were shredded, and my legs had several lacerations, but the blood was minimal. The heavy denim coat protected my upper body, but I had lost my cap somewhere. All in all, I was in good shape. My plan was to stick to the railroad tracks, jogging and walking until I reached a populated area, where I would call someone to come get me. It was October and the sun would rise around 7:15 a.m. If I hadn't been caught by then, I had probably gotten away unnoticed. The sun came up and I was still free.

I reached a populated area just north of Kansas City, Kansas, and started looking for a pay phone. I saw a phone outside a small business and went to it. Parked in front of the pay phone was a pickup truck, whose engine was running but unoccupied. I jumped in the driver's seat and took off. I headed for Kansas City, Missouri, and ten minutes later I was parked in front of a health club in Independence, Missouri. The pickup truck I had stolen was apparently a work truck, because I found a set of coveralls to hide my shredded clothing and a set of bolt cutters. I gained entrance to the health club by saying I had left my watch in the locker room the previous evening at closing time. The bolt cutters were easily hidden in my coveralls, and I was able to steal four wallets. I drove to a mall where I bought new clothing and got a haircut with the credit cards from a stolen wallet. I then went to a motel and rented a room, where I took a long, hot shower. I had several cuts and bruises, but nothing that required medical attention. All I needed was some dope, and to get out of town. I contacted my old dealer, who had just seen the story of my escape on the news and asked him to bring me some coke. He brought me an ounce of coke and $1,000 in cash. He advised me to leave Kansas City and to not look back. I thanked him and drove north to Chicago, where I was confident I could blend in.

While passing through Des Moines, Iowa, I stopped at a health club where I stole a wallet. Inside the wallet was the man's driver's license, and I noticed the photo on the license looked a lot like me. I used the stolen driver's license and a credit card to rent a mini-van and drove to Chicago. I met some people in Chicago who knew where to get cocaine, but not meth, so I spent the next couple of weeks shooting coke and stealing wallets.

I was paranoid beyond belief. Cocaine itself makes me paranoid, but when you add a constant fear of being caught, psychotic episodes were bound to occur, which they did. It was becoming more difficult to successfully complete a crime, because I felt as if everyone was watching me and wound up chickening out of committing crimes. I knew that I would eventually be caught and given a lot of prison time. I still had twenty-three years left of my twenty-five year sentence in Oklahoma, plus I would receive additional time for the escape from Oklahoma. I would also receive additional time for the escape from Kansas. My 40th birthday was coming up, and I felt that whenever I was captured, I would have more time to serve in prison than I had left on this Earth. My plan was to commit suicide whenever I was captured. I was captured three weeks after my arrival in Chicago.

CHAPTER 13

October 2000 – October 2009

At the end of October, I was arrested for theft at a health club in Lake County, Illinois (just north of Chicago). I also had cocaine in my possession, for which I was also charged. I gave the police my real name, and after a warrant check I was informed that both Oklahoma and Kansas had warrants out on me for escape. I believed that my life was over. I did not want to spend the rest of my life incarcerated, and even if I were released at some point in the future, what would I do? I began reflecting on the trauma of being raped in 1980 and all the misery and heartache that followed. Someone had hurt me and I, in turn, hurt everyone I encountered. I had made my family completely disown me. I had no friends. I never had any children (thank God). I was alone in the world, and no one would miss me if I were gone. The only thing I had to look forward to was the sweet release of death. My mind was made up.

On November 1, 2000, I asked a jailor for a disposable shaver so I could shave. I left my jail ID card with the jailor and went to my cell with the shaver. Once inside my cell, I broke open the shaver and removed the razor blade. I faced the stainless-steel mirror in my cell and began cutting my throat. I was trying to find my carotid artery, but no matter how deeply I cut, there was no blood spurting. I switched to the other side of my neck and began cutting again. I could feel the blade slicing through muscle in my neck, but still no blood spurting. I began cutting my wrists, one at a time, trying to find an artery. At this point I was, unknowingly, sobbing very loudly, which attracted the attention of some inmates outside my cell. They looked in through the window of my cell door, saw what I was doing, and called for help. Several officers entered my cell and handcuffed me. There was blood everywhere, but no spurting. I had failed.

I was taken to a hospital where surgery was performed to repair the muscles in my neck. Afterward, the surgeon told the Sheriff that my suicide attempt was the most serious unsuccessful suicide attempt he'd ever seen, and recommended I be place on suicide watch when I was returned to the jail. I was discharged from the hospital the next morning and returned to the Lake County Jail, where I was placed on high-risk suicide-watch.

I was housed in the "fishbowl," which was a cell with see-through plexiglass walls and a floor made from heavy duty rubber. There was no bed, no toilet, no sink. My toilet was a hole in the floor, which could only be flushed from outside the cell by a jailor. (Did I mention the walls of my cell were see-through?). The only clothing I was allowed was a "turtle suit," which was a specially sewn smock that could not be torn to prevent hanging oneself. I slept on the floor with no blanket, no sheet, no pillow. I guess they figured this would help with my depression. After two weeks of suicide-watch, I was allowed to return to general-population. All I had to do was promise to not kill myself.

I had decided that I would try to escape again if I got the chance. I received a four year sentence in Illinois, of which I served eighteen months before being granted parole. Due to my escape history, I was housed in a high security facility, from which I could not escape. After receiving parole in Illinois, I was extradited to Muskogee, Oklahoma where I was prosecuted for the escape and received a three year sentence to run consecutive to the twenty-five year sentence. Not too bad, since I was expecting an additional twenty-five years. I was housed at the medium-security unit of the Lexington Correctional Center, and six years later, in May 2008, I was granted parole from my twenty-five year sentence to my three year sentence. In June 2009 I discharged my three year sentence and was "released" on parole. I was "released" to the custody of the Kansas Department of Corrections, from which I had escaped in October 2000.

Because of a "due process" error by the Kansas Department of Corrections regarding the hold, or detainer, they placed on me while I was incarcerated in Oklahoma, Kansas was unable to prosecute me for the escape. I only had to finish the eleven month sentence I was serving when I escaped. One hundred days later, on October 15, 2009, I was released from the Kansas Department of Corrections on parole. At this point I was on parole for Oklahoma for ten more years, and parole for Kansas for the next twelve months. I was released with $200, but nothing else. I was homeless and I didn't know anyone in the area, except for drug addicts, drug dealers, and prostitutes. After nine years it would be virtually impossible to find anyone I once knew. I reported to the parole office in Olathe, Kansas, hoping my parole officer would help.

CHAPTER 14

October 15, 2009 – November 3, 2009

I met my parole officer, who addressed me as Randy White. I explained to her that my real name was David Joyce, and that Randy White was the fake name I was in prison for using. She didn't care. My paperwork said my name was Randy White, so she called me Mr. White. I explained to her that I was homeless and had absolutely no resources. My parole officer told me to figure it out, because it wasn't her job to babysit me.

The only identification I had was my KDOC prison ID, which had the name Randy White on it. I had no birth certificate and no way to obtain a Kansas Identification Card. My parole officer printed out a temporary identification, but it also had the name Randy White on it. I reminded my parole officer that I went to prison for using that name, then asked why it was illegal to use that name before I went to prison, but legal to use the name after being released. Pointing out the hypocrisy of the situation must have angered her, because she called me a smart-ass.

My parole officer drove me to a homeless shelter in Kansas City, Missouri, and dropped me off. She told me to report to her office weekly for drug testing, then drove away. I got in line with the other homeless people and waited for the shelter to start letting people inside. About an hour later, the line started moving. My only possession was a legal envelope with some paperwork inside. I didn't have a change of clothes.

Due to limited bedspace at the shelter, not everyone was able to make it inside for the night, and I was told that if I wasn't in line by 3:30 p.m. every day, I probably wouldn't make it inside. If by some miracle I was able to find a job, I would have to be back here at the shelter by 3:30 or else sleep on the streets. I made it inside that night, but having no transportation of my own, I knew I wouldn't make it back in time every day.

I, and the other homeless people, went to a dayroom inside the shelter and watched TV while dinner was being prepared. The men were all talking so loudly that it was impossible to hear the TV, which reminded me of prison. At 6:00 p.m. we were led into the dining area and fed Hamburger Helper and Kool-Aid, which reminded me of prison. At 7:00 p.m. we were taken to a community shower, where showering was mandatory. My clothes and legal envelope were taken from me and put into a locker, then I was given a "night shirt" to wear to bed. The night shirt was a T-shirt that went down to my knees and looked like a nightgown. While I was showering, two feet from another man, I noticed the man next to me had a large wound on his lower leg. I asked him what happened, and he told me he had a staph infection. Water from his body was splashing off the floor onto my body. I was livid.

After showering we were assigned bunks beds to sleep in. There were twenty-four men in the room I was assigned to, and they were all talking like they had known each other for years. One man was coughing, sneezing, and wheezing, and when someone asked him how he was feeling, he said he thought had the flu, and that he was going to the free clinic in the morning. Another man offered to go with the man with the flu, since he had to get some Quell to get rid of his crabs.

I told myself that I was better off in prison. There was no way I was going to make it like this. I had about $150 left of my gate money, which I was planning to spend on thrift store clothing. While lying in bed that night I changed my mind. I would spend the rest of my money on bolt cutters and a gym bag. I would start stealing wallets first thing in the morning. I would stay in the homeless shelter that night, but the Marriott the next night.

I was very successful the next day. I stole a wallet and a car from a health club in Missouri, then drove to Kansas to use the credit cards. Then I stole a wallet and car from a health club in Kansas and drove to Missouri to use the credit cards. I kept going back and forth, stealing wallets, and purchasing items to trade for drugs. By 5:00 p.m. I had over $2,000 in cash, over $2,000 worth of new clothing, and over $20,000 worth of merchandise to trade. I checked into a Marriott hotel, took a long, hot shower, then ordered room service. No Hamburger Helper that night – bacon-wrapped filet mignon and rock lobster tail was on the menu for me.

I hadn't had sex in over nine years, and I was ready. I called an escort service, and they sent a prostitute to my room. I paid her $400 for sex, and we got naked. As I said, it had been over nine years since I'd had sex, so I didn't last very long, but I'm sure it was the best fifteen seconds of her life. Afterward I asked her if she knew where I could get some meth. She said no, but that she could get me some cocaine. I gave her another $200 to get me three grams of coke. She returned thirty minutes later with the coke and we both got high. She stayed the night and the next day she introduced me to her dealer. I told the dealer about my credit card hustle, and he bought all the merchandise I had purchased with the credit cards earlier. He also gave me a wish-list for additional items. I was right back where I left off nine years earlier, and the result was predictable. Twenty days after being released from prison, I was arrested in Missouri for stealing wallets and using stolen credit cards. I also had a quarter gram of cocaine in my pocket at the time of my arrest, which the police found and charged me with. While in jail in Harrison County Missouri, I was notified that theft and credit card charges had been filed against me in two additional

Missouri counties, as well as one county in Kansas. I also had holds on me for parole violations in Oklahoma and Kansas. I hadn't even been out for three weeks.

CHAPTER 15

November 2009 – March 22, 2015

I wound up pleading guilty to: possession of cocaine in Harrison County, MO, and receiving a four year sentence; felony theft in Clay County, MO, and receiving a four year sentence to run concurrently with Harrison County; and felony theft and credit card fraud in Platte County, MO, and receiving a seven year sentence to run concurrently with Harrison County and Clay County. I was transported to the Missouri Department of Corrections to serve my seven year sentence. I was granted parole in July 2012 and transported to the Oklahoma Department of Corrections to serve my parole violation.

In June 2011, I received a letter from my little sister for the first time ever. I was very excited to receive her letter. It felt good to know that a member of my family was reaching out to me. Unfortunately, the letter was to inform me that our mother had passed away. She had passed away in January 2010, and I was notified seventeen months later. My sister told me that no one in the family knew where I was at the time, but that was not true. I had written a letter to my older brother in November 2009 while in jail in Missouri, and I was still there in January 2010 when my mother passed away from cancer. This told me all I needed to know about how my family felt about me. My sister and I kept in touch sporadically after that, as she had legal problems of her own and was in and out of jail.

While incarcerated in Oklahoma, I filed an Interstate Agreement on Detainers, requesting that the state of Kansas prosecute me for all pending charges in their state. In January 2013, I was extradited to the Shawnee County Jail in Topeka, Kansas, and prosecuted for eleven counts of theft and credit card charges. I plead guilty to all charges and was sentenced to eleven sentences of eleven months each, all concurrent with each other, and concurrent with my Oklahoma parole violation. I was transported back to the Oklahoma Department of Corrections with no additional time to serve.

At this point, I had nine years remaining on my Oklahoma parole violation, but I was eligible for good time (time off for good behavior). In Oklahoma, good time is only awarded while in custody, so if I were to be granted parole again, no good time would be awarded while I was not in custody. With my good time, if I wasn't granted parole, I would be out in two more years. If I were granted parole, I would have to serve nine more years on parole. Thankfully, I was denied parole and forced to complete my sentence in custody.

With no more holds on me, I was allowed to transition from maximum security to medium security, then to minimum-security, then to work release in January 2015. Work release allows inmates to obtain real jobs in the community for a smoother transition back into society, and to save money for their release. I had my mind set on leaving the ultra-conservative state of Oklahoma and going to a place where they treated criminals better. Criminals are treated as victims in California, so that was my destination of choice. Since I was not planning to stay in Oklahoma upon my release, I was not allowed to go out and find a real job while in the work release facility. Instead, I was forced to wash dishes at the Oklahoma Highway Patrol Headquarters for $7.20 per month. My release date was March 20, 2015, and I would be released with the mandatory $200 and a bus ticket to wherever I wanted to go. I chose San Bernardino, California because I knew the area, the weather was warmer than the coastal areas, and because my dad lived near San Bernardino. If I was going to be homeless, I didn't want to freeze to death.

Approximately one month prior to my release from prison I began to experience extreme anxiety mixed with bouts of debilitating depression. There were days when I didn't get out of bed or eat food at all. I contemplated escape and suicide. I was afraid to get out of prison. After sharing 8' X 10' cells with murderers, rapists, child molesters, gang bangers, armed robbers, and even a goat-fucker, I was more afraid of getting out of prison than I was in prison. I had no idea how to live in the real world. I felt like I was about to jump out of an airplane without a parachute.

After decades of believing that my behavior was normal, I finally realized that I was mentally ill. Being incarcerated with people who were more mentally ill than I was made me feel like I wasn't that bad off. I had accepted that my life was one big cycle, and that it was my destiny. I used to refer to my incarcerations as an occupational hazard, and a chance to get healthy. Einstein said that doing the same thing over and over, while expecting a different result, is the definition of insanity. I must not have been insane, because I always expected to get caught and go to prison, but I was, undoubtedly, mentally ill.

About two weeks prior to my release, I signed up for sick call and spoke to a physician's assistant about my mental health. He informed me that no counseling was available at the work release facility, but he would write me a prescription for some anti-anxiety and anti-depression medications. The medications helped, but only because they made me sleep more, making time go by faster.

I knew there was no way I would be able to make it in the real world without help. I reached out to my sister, who was living with our disabled father at the time, and asked my sister to ask our father if I could stay with them when I got out. As soon as she said, "Dave is getting out of prison soon..." our father said, "Don't bring that motherfucker here." She didn't bother to ask him if I could stay there with them.

My father was a good man. He served his country during the Korean War, came home, and married a good woman. My father drove city buses and school buses in New York City for a living but raised his family on Long Island. He worked ten to twelve hours a day, while commuting sixty minutes to work, and sixty minutes home every day. He worked hard to put food on the table and paid his bills on time. He was a faithful and loving husband. His greatest strength was that he always did the right thing. He had kicked me out of his house many times and told me to never come back, but many times he had also let me back in his house after I was released from prison. I felt that if I asked him face to face for another chance, he would do the right thing.

I also knew that I had to do things differently this time. I just didn't know how. My last job was the telemarketing job I had while in the Colorado work release facility. Other than that, I had no work history or verifiable references. While I was working at the Oklahoma Highway Patrol, I asked a staff member if they could look up telemarketing jobs in Hemet, California, where my father lived. The staff member provided me with an ad for telemarketing for a solar company. The ad said they were hiring immediately and that no experience was necessary. I would have to lie on my application, so hopefully there would be no background check, and no reference check. At least I had a lead.

My biggest challenge, however, was changing my mindset. My father, at this point, was seventy-eight years old. He was a very conservative Republican who believed in honesty, integrity, honor, and hard work. I was fifty-four years old, and was a liar with no integrity, honor, or sense of hard work. I had never followed politics, but in prison most inmates rooted for Democrats at election time. Most prison systems are constantly overcrowded, and we knew that to relieve overcrowding, the Democrats would let people out early, and the Republicans would build more prisons. In fact, in 2008, the prison held a mock election where the inmates would cast votes for governor and president, and the Democrat candidates (Brad Henry and Barack Obama) received 97% of the votes. My case manager asked me what I thought about the results, and I said it proved that Democrats are cooler than Republicans. He laughed at me and told me that, maybe, if I became a Republican there would only be a 3% chance I'd come back to prison. I laughed at him and told him I would never be a Republican.

I remembered that conversation just prior to my release and decided to ask my father to teach me how to be a Republican. I would ask him to re-raise me, like I was a teenager. I had become indoctrinated into the prison mentality and needed to be re-programmed. I needed to be rehabilitated from prison rehabilitation.

I contacted my sister again and asked her if she knew of any place I could stay for a couple of weeks. She was able to convince her husband and his roommates to let me crash on their couch until I found a job. It was a start. My sister also agreed to pick me up at the bus station in San Bernardino and drive me to Hemet, where my dad lived and where the telemarketing job was.

The bus pulled into the Greyhound station in San Bernardino on Sunday afternoon, March 22, 2015. I exited the bus, lit up a cigarette, and began looking for my sister. I hadn't seen her in twenty years. I hoped I would recognize her if I saw her. I had not cut my hair in three years, and it hung past my shoulders, so I was also hoping she would recognize me.

CHAPTER 16

March 22, 2015 – April 2015

I found my sister easily. She looked just like my Aunt Kathy, so I knew it was her, but I still had to ask. She did not recognize me at first, but she recognized my voice, and knew it was me. We drove the thirty miles to Hemet and caught up on a few things. She told me that our father was disabled but was pretty much self-sufficient. He had COPD, spinal stenosis, neuropathy in his lower legs and peripheral artery disease (PAD). He was able to walk, but only with a walker, and only for short periods of time. He was able to bathe and use the restroom unassisted. He was a cook in the Army, so he could feed himself. He just could not leave the house alone. My sister did all the shopping, laundry, and housekeeping. She also drove him to his doctor's appointments at the VA Hospital, in Loma Linda, California. My father was also suffering from depression. My parents were married for over fifty-one years when my mother passed away in 2010, and my father was still grieving. He worshipped the ground my mother walked on.

My sister was married and split her time between living with our father and living with her husband, who lived elsewhere with a couple of roommates. We drove to her husband's house where I would be staying temporarily and began looking through the want-ads on Craigslist. I had no idea how to use the internet, so I let my sister do all the work. The solar telemarketing job was listed. The position was for an Appointment Setter and consisted of cold-calling homeowners and pitching solar power for their homes. The job paid $9/hour and was a full-time position. No experience was necessary, and they were hiring immediately. We went to a thrift store, where I purchased three pairs of pants, five button-up shirts, some underwear and socks, and a pair of shoes for about $50. We went to a grocery store where I purchased cereal, milk, bread, and lunch meats. My $200 release money was dwindling fast.

My sister created a résumé for me, which was pure fiction. I had a fake work history, but my brother-in-law and his roommates agreed to verify the false information if anyone should call. I had telemarketing experience, so I listed my telemarketing job from Colorado when I was at the work release facility there. I was very hopeful that I would get the job.

Luckily, my father had a copy of my birth certificate at his house, which my sister was able to find. First thing Monday morning I went to the DMV and obtained a California ID card. I also applied online for my Social Security card. On Tuesday I applied for the solar job and was interviewed and hired on the spot. I started work the following day. I had only been out for five days and was hired for the first job I applied for. I was elated. Later I found out why it was so easy for me to get hired: Telemarketing for solar in California is the worst job in the world. Homeowners were constantly barraged with telemarketing calls from solar companies, and the rejection was overwhelming.

After receiving my first paycheck two weeks later, I decided to go see my father. My sister told me that he did not want to see me, but I felt I had to. My sister and I argued about it for a while, but she relented and drove me to see my father.

My father lived in a fifty-five and over mobile home park and owned a double-wide mobile home. The mobile home was built in 1976 but was in relatively good condition. He and my mother bought that home in 2000 and chose that mobile home park because it had an 18-hole golf course, and they enjoyed golfing. My mother had also passed away in the house while on hospice. When my sister and I walked in the house, my father did not immediately see me, and when he did see me, he did not recognize me. He asked who I was, and I responded, "I am your son." When he realized it was me, he got very angry with my sister for bringing me there. I told him that I only came to visit. I told him I had been staying with my brother-in-law and that I had already found a job and received my first paycheck. He softened a little bit, and we began a conversation. I told him how sorry I was for his loss, and for not being there when my mom was sick and, ultimately, passed away. I told him how sorry I was for being such a terrible son, brother, and uncle. Before long, we were both in tears. I promised him that it would be different this time. He'd heard that before, and asked for details on how things would be different.

I could sense that I had a chance to persuade him into letting me stay with him, so I went for it. I explained to him that I was mentally ill from the lifestyle I had been living for the past thirty-five years. I did not tell him about the rape, but I explained how my addiction took control of my life and made me do things I would not normally do. Then I explained how spending over thirty years of my life incarcerated had affected me. I told him that the past thirty-four years had taught me a different version of normalcy, and that I needed to be reprogrammed.

I then asked him if he would be willing to reprogram me by letting me live with him and treating me like a teenager preparing to go into the world as an adult. I promised that I would do anything he said, without question. I told him that if someone didn't teach me how to be a responsible, law-abiding citizen, I wouldn't stand a chance. He put my promise to the test immediately. He told me to get a haircut and he would agree. My first instinct was to say no, but instead, I asked my sister if she had any hair clippers. She said she did, and I asked her to give me a crew-cut. I sat there in my father's kitchen with a towel over my shoulders while my sister gave me a boot camp haircut. Like I said, my hair hung past my shoulders, so the result was eye-opening. My father's mouth was agape the whole time. When my sister was finished, my dad said to me, "Welcome home." Those two words saved my life.

CHAPTER 17

My father told me I did not have to pay for rent or utilities, but I had to buy my own food. My dad was on a fixed income, collecting Social Security. His total income was about $1,500/month. His lot rent and utilities totaled about $900/month, which didn't leave much money for food, beer, wine, cigarettes, and dog grooming, but he was a master budgeter, and made it work. He also had approximately $10,000 in Certificates of Deposits (CDs) for emergencies. I would do my best to not be a financial burden to my father.

I told my father about the mock election in prison, and how my case manager suggested I become a Republican. I asked my father to teach me about politics, and since he watched Fox News Channel from 6 a.m. until noon daily, there was plenty to discuss. I did not have to be at work until 1 p.m., so I got an earful of conservative viewpoints. The only cable news channel I watched in prison was CNN, because James Earl Jones said it was "the most trusted name in news." I heard things on Fox News that were contrary to things I'd heard on CNN and asked my dad how two different "news" channels could report on the same story yet have different villains. He explained to me that cable news channels did not just report facts anymore. He explained editorializing, and how opinions were expressed in such a way that opinions sounded like facts. He told me about agendas and how agendas shape the way news is broadcast. Of course, the 2016 presidential election was just gearing up, and I was amazed at the contrast between the way Donald Trump was portrayed on CNN and Fox News. CNN called him a moron, and Fox News acted like he was the second coming of Christ. I found it very confusing, but also very entertaining, so I paid attention. My dad was very much a Trump supporter, but I was secretly rooting for Bernie Sanders.

On the outside, I was holding up pretty well, but inside, I was very uncomfortable. I was constantly afraid of saying something inappropriate and looking like a moron. Work was different because I was reading from a script, with very little ad lib. I avoided conversations with co-workers and ate my lunch alone every day. At times, I would doubt my ability to succeed in the free world, which caused me a great deal of stress and anxiety. There were several nights when I could not sleep, because I could not shut my thoughts out. The constant rejection while telemarketing was not helping my self-esteem issues, and I began to hate my job. I talked to my dad about it, and he told me to look for another job, but under no circumstances should I quit my current job until I found a new job. I started looking on Craigslist for a new job that day.

After two weeks at my telemarketing job, I opened a checking account at a local credit union, and four weeks after that, I was offered a "first-time-buyer's" auto loan for a new car by my credit union. By this time, I had obtained a valid California driver's license. I was pre-approved for up to $17,000 for a new vehicle, and after looking online for deals on new vehicles, I headed to the local Hyundai dealership, where I purchased a 2015 Hyundai Accent GS. All I had to do was sign my name. I heard the finance manager say that my interest rate would be 23.9%, but I had no idea if that was a good rate or not. (Turns out, it was the highest interest rate allowable by law.) My payments were over $400/month, but I felt like I was stealing the car – literally. I was proud of myself for this accomplishment, but this purchase also elevated my anxiety level. In addition to the car payments, I needed to pay car insurance monthly. I now had financial responsibilities, and that was new to me.

My dad told me that he wanted me to be open and honest with him about any thoughts or feelings that made me feel stress or anxiety, so I talked to him often. He was always calm and rational, always asked the right questions, and listened carefully. I told him about my difficulties sleeping and eating, and he suggested I go to a mental health clinic and speak to a professional. I had applied, and was approved, for Medi-Cal after my release, and mental health visits were covered.

After fifty minutes of talking with the psychologist, he recommended I be prescribed Xanax for my anxiety and Zoloft for my depression. I took the medications as prescribed, and they helped somewhat. I found myself sleeping twice as much, which equals half as much anxiety and depression. The problem was that I didn't feel like going to work. I even fell asleep at work one day. Then, my sister asked me if I smoked marijuana. I told her I hadn't really smoked any weed since the 1980s, but I'd be willing to try anything. She rolled a joint from her own stash and lit it up. Ten minutes later, I forgot why I ever had anxiety to begin with. I laughed…and laughed…and laughed. I hadn't laughed that much in the past thirty-five years combined. I believed I had found the cure for anxiety, and my dad was okay with me trying it.

I do not advocate for the use of marijuana for everyone, but in some cases, mine specifically, I believe it is a better option than pharmaceuticals. As for the safety issue, it is true that if not used responsibly, being under the influence of marijuana can be dangerous, especially if a person does not smoke weed often. That being said, the difference between a driver under the influence of alcohol and a driver under the influence of marijuana is this: a drunk driver will run a stop sign completely, potentially killing someone, whereas a person high on weed will stop for the stop sign, but then sit there and wait for the sign to turn green, potentially annoying other drivers. I have never seen an episode of COPS where a guy smoked too much weed and went home and beat up his wife and kids. As far as I know, no one has ever died from an overdose of weed. Paranoia, mild psychosis, and anxiety sometimes occur, but they also occur while drinking alcohol much more often.

So, I applied, and was approved, for a Medical Marijuana Recommendation (commonly known as a Marijuana Card). I went directly to a marijuana dispensary and was amazed when I walked inside. The display counters were set up like jewelry stores, with glass jars full of huge buds instead of watches and rings. The prices ranged from $5/gram to $50/gram, and I learned that you get what you pay for. Since I was new to smoking, the $10/gram stuff was good enough. After telling the "Budtender" that I wanted to be able to sleep at night and stay awake during the day, he recommended Indica for sleep and Sativa for daytime, and I bought three grams of each. The Budtender knew what he was talking about, because I felt great during the day and slept like a baby at night. My appointment setting neither got worse, nor better, but I didn't care about the rejection anymore. In fact, I found it very funny at times. The only time I did not smoke was when I knew I had to drive, and luckily, my place of employment was only a five minute walk from home. My favorite activity was watching TV comedy shows like *Impractical Jokers* and *Ridiculousness*. Laughter is the best medicine.

Things were going surprisingly well. I wasn't exactly making my mark on the world, but I was on an even keel. I felt secure with the way things were going, and my daily conversations with my father were very therapeutic for me. The psychologist I was seeing did not approve of my marijuana usage and urged me to keep taking the Xanax and Zoloft, saying I had to give the medications time. I told him it took less than one minute for the marijuana to completely erase any feelings of anxiety, and that my depression was virtually non-existent. He told me he couldn't help me if I didn't take the medications, and I told him that was fine, and that I would stop coming to therapy.

CHAPTER 18

April 2015 – January 2016

I was spending time learning how to use the internet, and I kept searching for information on my father's illnesses. One of these searches led me to a home care support website. People who were in-home caregivers shared stories on this site. Most dealt with the stress of taking care of a loved one who is disabled or diagnosed with a terminal illness. People commented, liked, and shared messages of support. I began to imagine what I would do if my sister moved out and it was up to me to care for my dad by myself. And what if he became more disabled? I felt empathy for these people who put their lives on hold to keep an elderly family member out of a nursing home.

I read a post by a woman named Jeri who had been taking care of her disabled mother since she was a teenager. Her mother was suffering from Polio and was bedridden. I commented on her post, which led to us chatting on a regular basis. I didn't think I would ever meet this woman, so I was open and honest with her about my past. Of course, I did not tell her about the rape. To this point in my life, I had told no one about the rape. Jeri was very empathetic and understanding. I felt comfortable chatting with her.

Turns out, we were both fans of the same TV shows. "Actuality" TV, not to be confused with "Reality" TV, shows people's actual reactions to situations, and is very funny to me. We would watch them together online at first, until I found out that she also lived in Hemet, Ca. Jeri shared a house with her mother, daughter, son-in-law, and grandson.

Four generations under one roof. I suggested we meet for coffee, which led to a first date, which led to a second date. After the second date, my dad asked me what my "intentions" were with this girl. He was so Old School. I told him that I felt very comfortable with her, and that I really liked her. He asked if we'd had sex yet, and I said no. He asked me if I would still spend time with her if sex was off the table, and I said yes, I would. This was the first woman I liked spending time with without having sex.

Neither of us made much money. I had my $9/hour telemarketing job, and Jeri was paid by Riverside County In-Home Supportive Services (IHSS) to take care of her mother. She supplemented her income by being a "Lunch Lady" at a nearby school district. We spent most of our time at my house watching TV, which we both were fine with. My dad instantly loved Jeri and encouraged her to come over more often. The fact that Jeri is an excellent cook didn't hurt matters either. We both liked each other, were attracted to each other, and felt comfortable with each other. Jeri moved in with me, my dad, and my sister a few months later.

Just before Thanksgiving, 2015, we started talking about finding new jobs. She did not enjoy working at the school anymore. Her kids were all adults and had been out of school for several years. My dad jokingly suggested a newspaper route, and I had recently seen a posting for a newspaper carrier on Craigslist, so I searched for it and found it. The hours were 2 a.m. until 6 a.m., seven days a week, and paid $700 every two weeks. The hours were great, because I planned to quit my telemarketing job, and I would only be gone while my dad was sleeping. I would be home all day in case he needed anything.

I would report to a warehouse about a mile from my house, where I would insert and bag the newspapers for my route. I would then drive my own vehicle to deliver the newspapers. I didn't even have to get out of the car. I just had to throw the papers in the driveways. Sounded pretty easy. I applied for the job and started the same night. I rode with a trainer for a few days, then set out on my own. Since I was an independent contractor, using my own vehicle, I was allowed to have a passenger. Jeri went with me every night and helped me prepare my papers, then read the route sheet to me while I drove. We formed a system, and it worked pretty well. After a couple of weeks, I began feeling comfortable driving my route. Most of my deliveries were in sparsely populated rural areas, with unlit dirt roads and two-lane county roads.

Then on December 13, 2015, at about 4:30 a.m., while Jeri and I were delivering my newspapers, I accidentally struck an 85-year-old pedestrian with my vehicle. The road we were driving on was a dark, two-lane county road, with a 45-mile-per-hour speed limit. An oncoming vehicle was approaching, and I dimmed my high beams. When that vehicle passed me, I turned my high beams back on. I immediately saw the man walking toward me in the middle of my lane of travel. I slammed on my brakes and swerved to the left, but I hit him with my passenger side mirror. I came to a stop, and we got out to check on the man I had just hit with my car.

He had a huge gash on the top of his head, but he was conscious and able to talk. It was December 13, and even though we were in Southern California, the temperature was about forty degrees. I took off my coat and covered the man up while Jeri called 911. While on the phone with the 911 dispatcher, the man was able to give us his name and address, and I was relieved because he looked like he was going to make it. A California Highway Patrol (CHP) Officer showed up about five minutes later, and EMS was not far behind. Jeri and I backed off, letting the paramedics do their jobs.

I told the CHP Officer what had happened. I was given a field sobriety test on the scene and passed. I was not under the influence of marijuana either. Jeri and I were shaken up, but after the CHP Officer completed his investigation, we continued to deliver the newspapers. I felt terribly about hitting that man, and I hoped he would make a full recovery.

Three days later I received a phone call from the CHP Officer who responded to the accident, and he asked me to come to the CHP station so we could recreate the accident in the parking lot. When I arrived, I asked the officer how the man I hit was doing. His exact words were, "I regret to inform you that the victim succumbed to his injuries." I didn't know what that meant, but it sounded bad. I asked, "What does that mean?" He then told me that the man had passed away in the hospital after having a stroke.

I have been in at least fifty fights in my life, and I have only been knocked out once. A guy caught me with a roundhouse punch to my jaw, which buckled my knees and dropped me like a sack of potatoes. Hearing that I had killed a man had the exact same effect. My knees buckled and I dropped to the floor. I laid there sobbing, on the verge of hyperventilating. Jeri came over to comfort me, and we sat there on the floor, crying together.

After we had gathered ourselves, the CHP Officer read me my Miranda rights. Since the man had passed away, the accident investigation turned into a homicide investigation. I was told there was a possibility I could be charged with vehicular homicide or involuntary manslaughter. I was devastated and scared. Not only did I take a life, but I could potentially go to prison because of it. Jeri and I cooperated with the investigation and recreated the accident for the CHP Officer. After the investigation was completed, it would be up to the District Attorney whether to charge me with a crime. After several weeks, it was determined that the pedestrian was 95% at fault, while 5% was my fault. No charges were filed, and I received no traffic tickets. To this day I feel terrible about what happened.

CHAPTER 19

February 2016 – December 2017

I wound up quitting my telemarketing job shortly after getting the newspaper job. I was only making $350/week, but it was enough to make my car payments and buy food. The job was seven nights a week, and I spent most of my free time at home, not spending money. Jeri took on her own newspaper route and quit her *lunch lady* job. She was spending most of her time at our house and it only made sense that she move in with me, my dad, and my sister. Jeri would go to her mom's house when she finished her paper route in the morning, where she and her daughter, Vanessa, would tend to Jeri's mother's needs. Things were working out well, and we were content.

By the summer of 2016, Jeri had taken over the preparation of our meals, and we both took care of the housework, yardwork, shopping, and taking my dad to his medical appointments at the VA Hospital. My sister was able to spend more time with her husband, and eventually moved back in with him. Jeri and I moved into my sister's bedroom, and the three of us became a family.

Also in the summer of 2016, I was able to move up in the newspaper business. I was offered a position delivering routes that had no carriers, which paid $12/hour plus thirty-five cents per mile, which came to approximately $600/week. I felt like a rich man. In fact, in November 2016, I went to a Chevrolet dealership and purchased a new 2016 Chevy Equinox so I would be able to carry and deliver more newspapers. I applied for credit and was approved. I also traded in my Hyundai, which I felt uncomfortable driving since the accident.

Jeri and I became very close, and I was very much in love with her. On Christmas Eve, 2016, I proposed to Jeri at work. I commissioned a graphic artist to make a fake newspaper front page. The headline read: JERI WILL YOU MARRY ME? Under the headline was a photo of me on one knee, holding a ring box. The owner of the distribution company brought the fake newspaper to Jeri and asked her if she'd seen this story on the front page. He handed her the fake newspaper, then pointed at me. I was behind her, on one knee, holding the ring box, in the exact spot where the photo on the front page was taken. I asked, "Jeri, will you marry me?" She started crying and said, "Yes." We got married on April 25, 2017, and we are still together.

I could never have imagined that I would be married, holding down a job, and staying away from drugs. I had applied for several higher paying jobs, but my lack of skills and my inability to pass a criminal background check were constantly holding me back. I enrolled in an online university and attempted to earn a degree, but since I was so inexperienced with a computer, I was forced to withdraw after just one semester. There were times when I would get frustrated over all the roadblocks. I still struggle with frustration and my inability to control it.

In prison when I would get frustrated, I would seek out a sex offender and use him as a punching bag. I would focus on men who liked to rape young boys, but a random child molester would suffice. I cannot do that out here in the free world, so I try to focus on how much better off I am now than I was nine years ago. I have also attended a few treatment programs, and the one plaque that seemed to be on every treatment center's wall was The Serenity Prayer. I am not a religious man, but this prayer has become my mantra: "God, grant me the serenity to accept the things I cannot change, the courage to change the things I can, and the wisdom to know the difference." It's the *knowing the difference* part that I struggle with.

CHAPTER 20

January 2018 – December 2018

I was still delivering newspapers, but I had been transferred to the Riverside distribution center, where I was making over $800/week. I was working 50 – 60 hours a week, but being an independent contractor, I was not paid overtime pay. Working seven nights a week takes a toll on a person's body and mind. On the rare occasions I would get a night off, I couldn't sleep. My body and mind were programmed to wake up at 11:00 p.m.

My dad was eight-one by this time. He had been smoking cigarettes for sixty-five years, and consuming alcohol (mostly beer and wine) since he was eighteen. Since my mother passed away in 2010, my dad had been drinking every day. Two or three beers during the afternoon and two glasses of wine after dinner. He had also been taking prescribed morphine every day for nearly ten years, and Gabapentin every day for about one year. He suffered from PAD, which severely restricted the blood-flow to his lower legs. One day he hit his foot on the corner of his bed frame and developed a small wound on top of his foot. With little to no blood-flow to his foot, the wound could not heal. His leg could have been saved with bypass surgery, but due to his age, his cigarette habit, and the fact that he did not exercise, bypass surgery was deemed too risky. In March 2018, the wound on my dad's foot became infected and needed to be amputated above the knee. I found it odd that bypass surgery was too risky, yet amputation was not.

It was at this point that Jeri began getting paid by Riverside County

IHSS to care for my father. Jeri had experience caring for disabled people, and she taught my dad how to transfer from a chair to a wheelchair, and from a wheelchair to the toilet seat. My dad had not exercised in a long time, and his arms became very weak very quickly with a manually operated wheelchair, so I requested a power chair from the VA. They refused to provide him with a power chair because they wanted him to use the muscles in his arms. I understood this, but I did not want to see my dad struggle. I didn't want to see his arms tremble from exertion. I had to get him a power chair, but even used ones are very expensive. So, I wrote a letter to President Trump, and mailed it to 1600 Pennsylvania Ave.

I appealed to President Trump to intervene with the VA on behalf of my father. I explained that my dad was an eighty-one year old disabled veteran who lived on Social Security, and that using the manually operated wheelchair was very painful to my dad because of arthritis in his shoulders. I also told him that the VA denied his request for a hospital bed for his bedroom, and that my wife, his caretaker, was only five feet tall and struggled to get my dad in and out of bed. I put my letter in an envelope, stamped it, and sent it off.

A few weeks later, a call came in for me on my dad's landline telephone from the Patient Advocate at the VA Hospital. My dad answered his telephone and after the caller identified himself, the caller asked to speak with me. My dad said, "I'm the patient, you can talk to me." The caller insisted on speaking with me, so my dad put me on the phone. I said, "This is David Joyce." The man asked me if I had written a letter to the White House, and I said yes. He then said, "I've been instructed to get a list of the medical supplies you need to take care of your father." I had been planning on voting for the first time in my life in 2020, and Donald J. Trump had just secured my vote.

The VA ordered a custom-made power chair for my dad, which would take months to build, so we were given a loaner power chair to use until the custom chair was delivered. We also received a brand-new hospital bed with more adjustment options than a dentist's chair. Along with the bed came a hoist to lift my dad completely out of bed on days when he was feeling weak. We also received wheelchair ramps. In addition to all of this, we received a $6,000 grant to make the house more wheelchair friendly. We tore up the carpet and put down hardwood floors and installed safety rails in the restroom and shower. We had the door frames widened to make it easier for the power chair to fit through. Wow! One letter from a former career criminal to the most powerful man in the world made my dad's life so much more comfortable. I should've asked for a limo and chauffeur to take me on my newspaper route. I could've stood up and thrown the papers out of the sunroof.

My dad was proud of me for writing to President Trump. He was giddy just thinking about President Trump reading a letter written by his son, about himself. President Trump was way too busy fending off hoaxes perpetrated by the Democrats to personally respond to my letter, but he made sure my dad was taken care of. I remember my dad calling his sister, my Aunt Kathy, and telling her about the letter and the VA calling and insisting on speaking to me. It wasn't often I saw my dad smile since I moved in with him, but he was beaming from ear to ear. I finally did something to make my father proud, and I hope it felt as good to him as it did to me.

My dad discovered that "phantom pain" is real. He'd had neuropathy in his legs for several years, which caused him a lot of pain. At first, he was relieved that the loss of his leg would at least cancel out the neuropathy pain, but that relief quickly faded. My dad was still experiencing the same amount of pain in a part of his body that didn't exist anymore. The human brain is very complex. I suggested that the doctors prescribe him a placebo and tell him that the pills were guaranteed to relieve the phantom pain. Using a phantom pill to treat a phantom pain made sense to me, but not to the VA. They said to give it some time and it would probably fade away.

My dad did not smoke marijuana. He was not opposed to it, but because of his COPD, he couldn't smoke weed without coughing violently after each hit. I had done some reading on CBD and saw that many people with phantom pain found relief with CBD, so I went to the neighborhood marijuana dispensary and purchased some CBD with THC, and without. I also bought a marijuana brownie for my dad. Since it was still morning, I gave him the CBD without THC, then left to run some errands. When I returned, my dad was smiling. I asked why he was smiling, and he told me that the phantom pain was gone. He had not experienced a single pain in over two hours. My dad usually napped from noon until 2 p.m., and he fell right to sleep at nap time.

He woke up to some phantom pain and put a few more drops of CBD under his tongue. Within fifteen minutes, the pain had vanished. Why does mainstream health care deny the medical benefits of CBD and THC to some patients? I believe the short answer to that is "Big Pharma," but don't get me started on them. That evening after dinner, I gave my dad ¼ of the brownie I had purchased at Weeds-R-Us, and waited to see the effect it would have on him. About fifteen minutes later, I heard him laughing. I went into the living room and saw that he was laughing at his Yorkie, "Little Guy." Little Guy was spinning in circles, begging for a treat. This was something he did on a daily basis, but I had never seen my dad laugh about it. Tears were running down my dad's cheeks, and the more he laughed, the more Little Guy spun around. My dad asked me why Little Guy was spinning around like that, and I told him that he wanted a treat. He said, "Oh, yeah. I forgot," then laughed even more. It was so good to see him laugh.

My dad used to have a great sense of humor. He was always cracking jokes or making witty remarks. And his laugh was contagious. When I was a kid, I would hear him in the other room laughing, and it would make me laugh. I would tell him jokes that were funny to a six-year-old (but not so much to adults) and he would roar with laughter. I missed his laugh, and I was happy the brownie was able to make him laugh again.

My dad had been suffering from depression since the day my mom passed away. They were married for fifty-one years when she passed away, and he still worshipped the ground she walked on. He still had her ashes in an urn on his dresser because he wanted her nearby. A couple of times, I heard him talking to her urn. There was no chance he would fully recover from his depression, but at least he was having periods of happiness, free of pain.

CHAPTER 21

January 2019 – October 19, 2019

In early January, my dad banged his right ankle on his power chair while he was transferring from his shower chair and developed a wound, which quickly became infected. I asked the Vascular Surgeon to perform bypass surgery before it was too late, and, again, they said that it would be too risky. I went to the Patient Advocate and threatened to notify President Trump about my dad's situation, and he said he'd look into it. The next day, the VA called to schedule a "vein-mapping" to see if my dad had any viable veins to use for bypass surgery. The mere threat of contacting President Trump was enough for the Vascular Surgeon to change her mind. Unfortunately, my dad had no viable veins to use. In April 2019, my dad had his right leg amputated above the knee.

Luckily, he had become adept at transferring from one chair to another, and my dad was a true soldier. He grunted through the pain and moved forward. The level of care he needed didn't really increase, nor did his pain level. I gave him regular CBD every morning, and CBD with THC before bed. He was also taking morphine and Gabapentin, so he wasn't really feeling much pain at all.

On August 23, 2019, my dad was watching TV in his living room, while Jeri and I were in the other living room. I went to check on my dad and saw him fumbling with his TV remote control. I asked him what he was trying to watch, and he said he didn't know. I thought that was an odd response, but before I could follow up with another question, Little Guy started spinning in circles and woofing for a treat. My dad asked why the dog was acting like that, and I told him that Little Guy wanted a treat. My dad asked where the treats were, and I said they were right in front of him on the countertop. But instead of grabbing the treat jar, my dad grabbed his morphine bottle and tried to give Little Guy a morphine pill. I took the pill bottle from him and asked him if he felt ok. He said yes, but that he was tired. It was only 7 p.m., but he obviously needed some sleep. I didn't give him any CBD that night, and we kept checking on him to make sure he was breathing. Jeri called in sick and stayed with my dad while I went to work.

The next day, my dad was having trouble remembering everyday things. We called the VA and asked if we could bring him into the ER. They said yes, and off we went. They performed a CAT scan to rule out strokes, and the scan was negative. They said that his medications needed to be adjusted and he should be fine in a few days. We took him home and waited. A few days later, we noticed a significant worsening of his memory and ability to form words, so we took him back to the ER. They performed another CAT scan, which was negative. They said to give it more time.

A week later, my dad could barely speak or move his arms. We insisted on a consultation with a specialist and two weeks later attended the appointment. They did a CAT scan on my dad and discovered that he'd had three mini strokes recently. He was diagnosed with Vascular Dementia, which is just like regular Dementia, except Vascular Dementia progresses much more aggressively.

It wasn't long before my dad lost the ability to communicate completely. He also lost control of his motor skills. Jeri and I arranged our schedules so that one of us would always be at home and awake. I quit my newspaper job and got a day job delivering auto parts in the morning, and marijuana in the afternoon (for the same 3rd party delivery service). We had to do everything for my dad. We spoon-fed him, bathed him, and changed his adult diapers. Eventually, my dad was no longer able to swallow food or water. On October 18, 2019, we took him to the ER at Hemet Hospital because his breathing was very labored. It was determined that his organs were full of infections, and there was nothing they could do except to rehydrate him and make him comfortable. My brother and I decided to bring him home on hospice.

My dad said many times that he did not want to die in a hospital. He wanted to die at home in his bed, in the same room where my mom had passed away. On October 19, 2019, at 2:30 p.m., we took my dad home and put him into bed. The hospice nurse inserted an IV into my dad's arm and gave him morphine. Jeri and I sat with my dad, each of us holding one of his hands. At 3:15 pm, my dad stopped breathing. The hospice nurse checked his vitals and told us that he was gone. The world lost a good man that day.

CHAPTER 22

October 20, 2019 – December 31, 2019

I was eleven days from turning fifty-nine, and I had never been to a funeral. My grandparents all passed away while I was young, and I had never experienced grief until I found out about my mother's death. My mother's death was surreal to me. She had been gone for seventeen months by the time I found out, plus the relationship I had with my mother while she was alive was not a good one. I mourned her death, but it did not paralyze me. My dad's death, however, hit me hard. I bawled like a baby for at least an hour before I ran out of tears. Jeri and I just cried and held each other. Jeri never knew her father, and over the past four and a half years had begun to look at my dad as her father as well. My dad, of course, considered Jeri his daughter.

Jeri's main income was for taking care of my dad, and now that he was gone, Jeri was unemployed. Jeri's daughter was receiving the pay for taking care of Jeri's mother. She still had her newspaper job, but that only paid $250/week. My dad was paying the lot rent at the mobile home park, plus all the utilities with his Social Security check. That was now gone. My dad left his house to me and my two brothers. The valuation of the house, because of its age, was only $18,000. I had to come up with $12,000 to buy my brothers out. I took out a $6,000 personal loan to pay one of my brothers and paid the other with a credit card. Life had just become much more challenging, financially, for me and Jeri. What else could possibly go wrong?

On December 5, 2019, Jeri's mother passed away. I had only met Jeri's mother a couple of times, as she had been bedridden for years. I had been working seven nights a week, 50 – 60 hours a week, and when I wasn't working, I was at home. Jeri was experiencing more grief than I was because she was much closer to my dad than I was to her mom. She felt as if she had just lost both of her parents in a six week period. Our losses deeply affected both of us, and our relationship became strained. We went through a couple of rough patches in our relationship, but we are still together.

Living with my dad provided me with a great sense of security. Without him, I would have been back in prison within six months. He was now gone, and I felt like an eighteen-year-old moving out of his parents' house for the first time. Had I not been clean and sober for so long, this may not have been a test I would've passed. The pain I felt from the loss of my father was overwhelming at first. My heart literally ached. I felt as if I had absorbed my dad's phantom leg pain into my heart. But, time passes, and the pain eases. I still miss my dad very much. I, like my dad, am having trouble letting go of ashes. I still have my dad's and my mom's ashes, in their respective urns, right here next to my desk. A photo of my dad is the screensaver on my phone. And I still have his dog, Little Guy.

After losing my dad and Jeri's mom, 2019 ended in depression for us. Surely 2020 would be better, right?

CHAPTER 23

January 2020 – December 2020

J eri began collecting unemployment after our parents passed away, and I continued to deliver auto parts and weed. Our budget was tight, but at least we were homeowners. We had adopted two dogs from a couple who were moving and could not take their dogs with them. Buddy, a four-year-old Bassett Hound, and Molly, a five-year-old Yorkie-poo became a part of our family in May 2020. Jeri was looking for a job to replace her IHSS job but wasn't having much luck. I had filed a lawsuit against the newspaper distribution company for back pay, and in retaliation, Jeri was let go from her newspaper delivery job. And then Covid hit. Suddenly, Jeri was being paid $1,000/week to stay home. She would have to work forty hours/week at $25/hour to make $1,000. Why work?

Believe it or not, delivering marijuana was considered "essential" in California during Covid, so not only was I still working, but also getting 10 – 20 hours per week overtime. People couldn't go to bars, so they stayed home and smoked weed. I was constantly teasing Jeri about being a Democrat, living off government handouts, but to be honest, I secretly wished I was getting paid $1,000/week to stay home.

By October, Jeri's unemployment was running out, so she got a job delivering packages for UPS. She was still making $1,000/week, but now she was working forty hours a week to get it. The job with UPS was a seasonal position, which ended right after Christmas. My company was hiring drivers with their own pick-up trucks, so Jeri and I went to a Ford dealership and bought Jeri a 2020 Ford Ranger. My boss hired Jeri the next day.

The country was being torn apart in 2020, but between the stimulus checks and the unemployment benefits, we made it through the year virtually unscathed. Jeri and I picked up the pieces of our lives and moved forward. In November 2020, I voted for the first time in my life. I had been paying attention to politics, mostly via social media. I began to notice that if a person posted anything with a conservative view, that person was immediately attacked. I was careful about the things I posted on Facebook, but a couple of times I made conservative comments to other people's posts, and people who knew nothing about me were calling me a piece of shit, with one person wishing I would catch Covid and die. By the end of the year, Jeri and I had deleted our social media accounts.

Our mobile home was located inside a fifty-five and over gated community, with security guards, in Hemet, California. On December 31st, at 5:00 a.m., I was about to take my dogs to the dog park when I heard noises from the bed of my 2018 Ford F-150. I looked into the bed of my truck and saw two men performing oral sex on each other, simultaneously. I had once walked into my prison cell and caught my cellmate kissing another man on my bunk, and I went ballistic. I beat my cellmate unconscious without even thinking about what I was doing. My cellmate spent two weeks in the hospital, and I spent 6 months in the hole (solitary confinement). When I saw these two men in the bed of my truck, my first instinct was to go ballistic, but I caught myself. I thought about the possible consequences, and the things I would lose if I was to beat someone unconscious. Instead, I yelled, "HEY!" The men looked at me and said, "Oh shit" at the same time. I told them to get the fuck out of my truck, which they did. They ran down my driveway and scaled the four-foot wall to the street. This was too much. We had to get out of California.

My brother, Chris, had moved to Texas a few years before, and had nothing but good things to say about the state. Jeri and I were two conservatives living in Liberal Mecca, so we began getting our house into selling condition, and making plans to move to Texas. Both my mother and my father had passed away in that house, and I had no intention of following in their footsteps.

CHAPTER 24

January 2021 – December 2021

J eri and I spent the next several months making repairs on the house as we could afford it. Our washer, dryer, and refrigerator all broke down in the same week. All three of those appliances were twenty years old, so we replaced them all with new ones. Then, Buddy developed bladder stones and required a $6,000 surgery. Things were not going well for us financially, but we were getting by. We ate ramen noodles for dinner six nights a week, cereal for breakfast, and sandwiches for lunch. We were both suffering from depression and had both lost our appetites anyway.

I felt like I was going backward and needed to do something progressive. Soon after my release from prison in 2015, my older brother told me that he'd done a genealogy DNA test. For all her life, my mother believed that she was Native American. She had black hair, brown eyes, and high cheek bones. She looked Native American. Turns out, my brother had no Native American blood at all, but he was 8% African, from the Ghana region. In the summer of 2021, I had a genealogy DNA test done myself, and found that I am 5% African, from the Ghana region. By this time, I had already denounced white supremacy, but I still had the WHITE PRIDE tattoos. On my 61st birthday, I went to a tattoo shop and covered up the tattoos with black redaction bars.

What people don't realize is how big of a step that was for me. Most people have said that it was about time I covered the tattoos up, and that I never should have had the tattoos to begin with. Both statements are correct, but to me it meant more. Voluntarily covering up tattoos like that would completely ostracize me from the Whiteboys in prison, so voluntarily covering up my tattoos was a statement to myself. It was like having confirmation that my old life was behind me. My only regret is that I didn't do it while my dad was still alive.

In mid-November, my brother, Chris, invited me to his wedding in Georgetown, Texas, which was scheduled for December 11. Jeri and I needed a vacation and accepted my brother's invitation. We scheduled a week off from work and drove from Southern California to Central Texas (with our three dogs). The drive was two days each way, so we only had three days of actual vacation, but we had a great time. The wedding was very nice, and my brother asked me to make the toast. I felt honored. My brother, Chris, was the hardest sell on my potential rehabilitation in the beginning, but over the six years since my release, he became a believer in me. It felt good to do a "big brother" thing.

We had such a good time in Texas that we decided to get serious about moving. Everything was less expensive in Texas than in California. Gas in California at this time was over $5/gallon. It was only $2.50 in Texas. Renting a three-bedroom duplex in California would cost about $3,000/month. Here in Texas, we pay less than $1,500/month. We scouted out jobs while we were in Texas, and found job openings delivering auto parts, and delivering newspapers. We decided to take the leap.

CHAPTER 25

January 2022 –

On January 2nd we hired a real estate agent to help us sell our house. On March 3rd, we closed escrow on our house for $36,000, loaded our two pickup trucks and one small trailer with our belongings, and began our exodus from the *land of fruits and nuts*. We didn't take any of our furniture, nor our bed. We either gave away, sold, or simply left in the house (with the buyer's permission) everything that didn't fit in our trucks and trailer.

Two days later, we arrived in Georgetown, Texas, checked into a motel, and started looking for a place to rent. We had been in contact with an independent delivery company in Georgetown prior to our move, and both Jeri and I were guaranteed jobs upon our arrival. After a few days, Jeri and I found a three-bedroom duplex in a small town outside of Georgetown. It was a two-story place with a fenced backyard. Our dogs were used to a small patio at our mobile home, and this yard was a perfect size for our dogs. Our drive to work would only take about twenty minutes. It was perfect. We signed the lease the next day and moved in that night.

We both delivered auto parts during the day, and to supplement our income, I took a side job delivering newspapers. I took a small route that paid $500/week, and since it is an independent contractor position, Jeri and I split the route. We reported to work at 2 a.m. and were both home by 5:00 a.m. We went home, took a nap, then reported to our day jobs at 9:00 a.m. Things were working out well.

In June, we were offered new, longer routes (one for me, one for Jeri), which paid more money. As a newspaper carrier, you are paid per paper delivered, so the more papers you deliver, the more money you make. The problem was that my route was so long that there were days I was not able to make it to my day job on time. Jeri's route was shorter than mine, so it wasn't as much of a problem for her. My newspaper job paid about $200/week more than the auto parts job, so I left the auto parts job. Jeri continues to deliver newspapers at night, and auto parts during the day. I deliver newspapers at night, and take care of the housework, yard work, shopping, vet appointments, etc. I told Jeri I would cook, but the only things on the menu would be ramen noodles, sandwiches, and cereal. Jeri said she'd handle the cooking.

Since we didn't bring any furniture with us, we bought all new furniture. We also bought a washer and dryer, a riding mower, and a TV. After using the proceeds from the sale of our house to pay off all of our debts and buy new furniture, we were broke again, but we had no debt. From March 2015 until March 2021, I paid $50/month to The State of Oklahoma for my court costs and fines, and never missed a payment. In March 2021, I paid the balance of my debt to The State of Oklahoma. Being debt-free, however, was short-lived. Both of our vehicles had over 100,000 miles on them and were out of warranty. The vehicle repair costs were adding up, and then Little Guy needed knee surgery for a luxating patella. Two months later, he needed the same surgery on the other knee. Two months after that, Buddy needed his gall bladder removed. I only make about $40,000/year (before taxes and vehicle expenses, like gas) and those three surgeries cost us $30,000. Our vehicle repair bills totaled $10,000 for the year. It was like we were stuck in the mud with our wheels spinning, but not going anywhere.

When I begin to get discouraged with the way my life is going, I follow my dad's advice and compare my life now to how my life would be if I were in prison. I keep putting one foot in front of the other and plodding on. Looking back on my life, I wonder how I stayed alive for so long. I believe that I am still here on this Earth for a reason, and I believe that reason is for me to help others avoid getting caught in the same cycle I was in for so many years. I am constantly sending emails volunteering to share my story with young people, but, unfortunately, most places want volunteers to be out of prison and off supervision for ten years. I still have a year and a half to go, so I decided to write this book. I hope my story helps someone struggling with drug addiction, recidivism, PTSD, or other mental illnesses.

CHAPTER 26

The Early Years

I don't want to give anyone the impression that I was an angel prior to my rape, and subsequent addiction, because I was not. I was born and raised on Long Island, New York. I have three siblings: Don Jr., one year older than me; Chris, three years younger than me; Sharon, seven years younger than me. My father was a bus driver in New York City, and my mother was a stay-at-home mom. Our family lived paycheck to paycheck, and we attended public school. From age seven to age seventeen, we lived in a town called Hicksville. Hicksville's claim to fame is being the hometown of Billy Joel. Hicksville was a blue-collar, lower middle-class town, and growing up in the 1960s and 1970s was an interesting time.

During the '60s and '70s, the New York Police Department was at its peak of corruption. Because of this corruption, my parents discouraged us kids from becoming police officers. Then, in 1975, the Vietnam War ended. I remember seeing on the news how civilians here in the US were spitting on our soldiers returning home from the war. All I heard on the news was how our soldiers were raping and killing women and children in Vietnam and burning down entire villages of civilians. My dad, who was a Korean War Era Veteran, had always spoken highly of his military experience, and wanted me to join the Army after high school. After the Vietnam Era, and seeing the way our soldiers were treated, we decided that maybe the military would not be the best choice. I had no idea what career path I would choose, but I would not join law enforcement, nor the military.

My parents were strict, but looking back now, I believe they could have been stricter. We all had bedtimes, curfews, and chores. My parents were both registered Democrats, but that was when the Democrats actually helped the middle-class. Back when their slogan was, "Ask not what your country can do for you – ask what you can do for your country." My parents instilled (what would now be considered conservative) values in us. Honesty, hard work, responsibility/accountability, manners, courteousness, and respect for others were things my parents emphasized. I went along with the program until I was fifteen years old.

In December 1975, I drank alcohol for the first time. My friend's mother was throwing a Christmas party and my friend and I decided to add vodka to our orange juice when no one was looking. Our drinks were half vodka and half orange juice. One glass each was enough to get us drunk, but we went back for seconds. About halfway through our second glasses, we started vomiting. My dad was called and left his own Christmas party to come get me. Luckily, we were only two houses away, and he was able to carry me home and put me to bed.

I got grounded for a month for drinking alcohol and took two days to recover from being drunk. You would think that I would be done with alcohol. Nothing good had come from drinking. Yet, I continued to drink alcohol at any chance I got. If I could pinpoint the period of my life when things changed for the worse, it would be this period.

I began to make new friends and acquaintances who not only drank alcohol, but also smoked marijuana. It wasn't long before I tried weed for the first time. The high was okay, but I preferred alcohol. I've heard from "professionals" for many years that marijuana is a "gateway drug" which leads to harder drugs. That statement may be true in many cases, but I believe that in most cases alcohol usage precedes marijuana usage. So, which one is actually the gateway drug? I believe it is alcohol. Alcohol was much easier for me to get than weed, and I believe that to be the case today. It's hard for parents to tell their children to not drink alcohol when they themselves drink alcohol. I began smoking cigarettes after I started drinking, and my parents were livid. But how could they tell me not to drink or smoke when they both drank and smoked in front of us kids and inside our house? I became rebellious and started making very bad decisions.

In the summer of 1977, at age sixteen, my friend and I decided to steal a car from Jones Beach, where we had been swimming all day. My friend had keys to a 1965 Chevy Impala he used to own, and those keys fit virtually every other 1965 Impala. The keys worked in the very first 1965 Impala we saw, and we took off. In the glove box was a quarter ounce of marijuana and a wallet containing $150. We went to the nearest mall and bought new clothes. While putting on the new clothes in the parking lot of the mall, we were spotted by two undercover officers who suspected we were shoplifters. When we drove away, the unmarked police car got behind us and pulled us over. My friend and I both got out and ran but didn't get far before we were apprehended. I, of course, still had the weed we found in the car on me. I was charged with unauthorized use of a vehicle and possession of marijuana. I ultimately pleaded guilty and was sentenced to probation by the courts, and was grounded until my 18th birthday by my parents. You would think that I would have learned my lesson.

In November 1977, at age seventeen, I was arrested for the sale of marijuana. I had sold a girl $10 worth of weed, and we went behind the mall to smoke a joint when the cops rolled up on us. She was arrested for possession of marijuana and when she was asked where she got it, she told them she bought it from me. I pleaded guilty to disorderly conduct and was sentenced to stricter probation, which consisted of more frequent probation office visits and drug testing.

In January 1978, in my senior year, I dropped out of high school to pursue a career working at McDonald's. My parents tried and tried to convince me to stay in school, but it was hard to drink alcohol at school without getting caught, and drinking alcohol was very important to me. My parents had had enough of me and told me to move out. I found a room for rent nearby and began my life as an adult.

In June 1978, my parents decided to move to San Diego, California, and I was able to convince them to let me move with them. I made a deal with my parents that if after six months in California, I did not have a job and my own place to live, I would join the military. My dad had checked with a recruiter and was assured that even with my criminal record, I would be allowed to enlist with some kind of waiver.

I was able to find a job as a delivery driver quickly and began saving money. I had stopped drinking alcohol and smoking marijuana. I met a nice girl and began a relationship with her. Within six months of my arrival in California, my girlfriend and I rented an apartment. I did not have to join the military. The night we moved into our new apartment, my girlfriend and I threw a party, where I drank beer and smoked weed. I did not get drunk or smoked-out, and I felt okay the next day. I decided that I would restrict my drinking and smoking to the weekends and was able to stick to that until the rape.

CHAPTER 27

The Cycle

There are basic methods of learning in life, one of which is associating bad behavior with negative consequences. Most people do something bad, suffer negative consequences, then stop doing whatever behavior caused the negative consequences. Common sense, right? Some people, however, continue to behave badly, knowing they will suffer negative consequences. Those are the people who are easily caught up in the cycle of addiction and recidivism. Not only was I one of those people, but I spent my entire adult life surrounded by people like that.

Drugs can make a person feel good and drugs can make a person feel bad. Addicts never seem to remember the bad times but are eternally optimistic about attaining the same feeling they got the first time they got high, which is rarely the case. The first time I used meth I had a very good experience, and from that time on, I was always trying to duplicate the feeling. I wanted that feeling of elation 24/7. At first, I told myself that the meth was necessary to avoid the nightmares, like medicine. Eventually, however, I became a full-blown addict, and the meth became mentally necessary. Being high on meth became normal to me.

Supporting a drug habit on minimum wage was impossible, so stealing became my job. I knew that eventually I would be caught and suffer negative consequences, but I did not care at the time. Of course, when I got caught, I would be like everyone on the TV show COPS when they get arrested. I would cry and plead with the cop not to arrest me and feel like it's the end of the world. But after several arrests, I began to accept that being arrested was part of my life. In fact, there were several times that I was relieved by being arrested. Many times, I needed to get healthy, and jail/prison provided me with nutrition and sleep. That kind of thinking comes with mental illness.

The more times I was incarcerated, the more comfortable I became with institutional living. I learned the ropes from older convicts and began to mimic their ways. Once I put on some weight and started lifting weights, I became a bully. If I found out that someone was a child molester or a snitch, I would take any commissary items they had, and if they put up a fight, I would beat the shit out of them. Most of the time, I would get snitched off and go to segregation for thirty days or so, but when I would get out of the hole, I would receive praise from the other inmates (and even staff sometimes). Out in the free world, people like me were not respected at all, but in prison I got a lot of respect. I felt important in prison, which added to my mental health issues, and contributed to the cycle.

The prison mentality develops very quickly, mostly because of the immediate negative consequences of negative behavior doled out by other inmates. When I say "negative behavior" I mean things like: sitting on the wrong side of the chow hall; talking to a correctional officer in private; hanging out with a sex offender; talking too loudly while someone is sleeping nearby and not brushing your teeth before going to breakfast. All these things come with a beat-down, or at least a "chin-check" (one punch to the chin). Even if you are not the person committing the "offense," you still learn. If a person is a documented snitch or child molester, that person risks their life every single day in general population.

In 2014, while I was incarcerated at the James Crabtree Correctional Center in Helena, Oklahoma, an inmate was having a bad day. I believe he was expecting his girlfriend to visit him, but she never showed up. He was so angry about being stood up that he stabbed a child molester to death. He admitted to the stabbing and said he had done the world a favor by ridding the world of a "chomo" (child molester). Two days later there was an article in one of the newspapers about the murder. Turns out, the inmate who committed the murder was, in fact, a child molester himself. He had kidnapped, raped, and murdered a fourteen-year-old girl in Missouri, and was sentenced to life in prison in Missouri. After several attempts on his life in the Missouri Department of Corrections, he was sent to the Oklahoma Department of Corrections for his own protection.

In 1984, while incarcerated in the California Department of Corrections, I witnessed a man's head caved in with a steel pipe because he cheated during a game of pinochle. The man who committed the assault was my pinochle partner, and we were cheating also. My pinochle partner almost killed someone for doing something we ourselves were doing. I was supposed to do the same thing to the victim's pinochle partner, but he immediately ran when my partner produced the steel pipe. When I saw my partner hit the other inmate (from behind) with the pipe, I momentarily froze. The dayroom where we were playing cards emptied in a hurry. No one wanted to be next, and no one wanted to be called as a witness later. I had a steel pipe in my waistband that I needed to get rid of, so I took off also. The assaulted inmate did not die, the assaulter was sent to San Quentin, and I was not even questioned. I did, however, stop cheating at pinochle after that incident.

The lessons learned in prison are sometimes a matter of life or death. People who come to prison are already emotionally and mentally damaged, and many are unpredictable. Prison life can be brutal to the psyche. Fighting is something that inmates must do, or risk becoming a "punk." If an inmate comes into another inmate's cell and demands all the inmate's commissary, the inmate either fights to keep his property, or gives it up without a fight and earns the label of "punk." If that inmate snitches on the other inmate, he becomes a "punk-ass-snitch," and must go to protective custody or forever have his commissary taken from him. The inmate's third option is to become someone's "bitch," meaning girlfriend, and be protected by his "daddy."

To survive in prison, one must be tough, physically and mentally. Kindness is perceived as weakness, and eventually one forgets how to be kind. Inmates sit around telling stories about selling drugs, committing robberies and burglaries, having sex with multiple women, owning jewelry and nice cars. Nobody talks about how their lifestyles are affecting their loved ones. Nobody talks about getting a job and supporting their kids or being a better husband. Inmates may think about those things, but talking about them is considered a sign of weakness.

The longer a person is incarcerated, the more damaged that person becomes. Their way of life becomes normal to them, and very few inmates have the opportunity to properly transition back into society. Inmates are normally classified into groups, and each group is treated differently. Violent offenders are treated differently than non-violent offenders, and sex offenders are treated differently than regular violent offenders. Each group of offenders, however, is treated the same within the group. For example, all non-violent offenders are treated the same as each other, even though the needs of each individual non-violent offender may vary.

Prior to my release in 2015, my case manager knew I was going to be homeless, and that I did not want to reside in Oklahoma. I was housed at a work-release center, but instead of allowing me to find a real job so I could save some money for my release, my case manager refused to let me find a real job in the community because of my escape history. If I was still an escape risk, why was I at a work-release center? Being released from prison after spending thirty of the previous thirty-four years incarcerated with no solid release plan was utterly irresponsible on the part of the Oklahoma Department of Corrections. Though I had a few case managers along the way that cared about the actual "correction" of bad behavior, most correctional staff are overworked, understaffed, and underpaid, creating an attitude of apathy among staff.

After years of institutional living, inmates must be transitioned back into society. Inmates must be treated as individuals to address individual needs. Many inmates are beyond rehabilitation, mainly because in order to be RE-habilitated, one must have at some point been habilitated. Many inmates do not want help, so the help should be focused on the ones who want help. For years, I did not want help. I only wanted to get out so I could pick up where I left off prior to my arrest. I'm not saying that some people should not serve long sentences. I have shared 8 x 10 cells with murderers, rapists, child molesters, domestic abusers, etc., who need to be incarcerated for long periods of time. There is no answer to criminal justice reform, but if the system would focus on the inmates who want help, the system will improve.

Once a person is caught up in the criminal justice system, a cycle begins. Drugs, crime, incarceration, freedom; drugs, crime, incarceration, freedom; drugs, crime, incarceration, freedom, etc. Breaking that cycle and learning how to live in society has been more mentally challenging than learning how to survive in prison. Inmates reentering society need to learn that it's okay to be kind and courteous to other people. They need to be taught about current events and how to navigate the internet. They need cell phones. They need healthcare. They need vehicles and driver's licenses. It would cost a lot less to keep a former inmate out of prison than to keep him in prison. It costs, on average, about $22,000/year to incarcerate an inmate in a state prison for one year. If $22,000/year was allotted for each inmate for three years after their release, the former inmate would have a chance. Allow the parole officer to control the money but make it available for the needs of the newly released inmate.

I have been a free man for eight and one half years, but still have moments when my prison mentality instinctively kicks in, especially when I feel someone has disrespected me. I have not assaulted anyone since my release, but I have come close several times. I sometimes have trouble controlling the words that come out of my mouth when I get angry and use the word "motherfucker" a lot. My prison instincts have subsided over the years, but I have a hard time socializing for fear of saying or doing something embarrassing. I should be in therapy, but delivering newspapers is not a job that comes with health insurance, and I cannot afford to purchase my own health insurance. And because of my past, as well as my age and physical limitations, I am resigned to working minimum wage jobs until I'm seventy and hoping that Social Security benefits will still be available in seven years.

Though I still have mental issues to deal with, I can safely, and honestly, say that I have broken the cycle of addiction and recidivism. I would like to give credit to my father and my wife for putting up with a trainwreck like me, and apologize to everyone whose life I have negatively affected.

Made in the USA
Middletown, DE
02 August 2024